VOLUME 10   GAT-KIT

THE PRACTICAL ENCYCLOPEDIA OF
Good Decorating
and Home Improvement

GREYSTONE PRESS

Alphabetically arranged and fully illustrated, your *Practical Encyclopedia of Good Decorating and Home Improvement* has been planned for your convenience and immediate use. In feature articles you will find a wealth of facts, ideas, suggestions, and advice that will help you solve your decorating problems. A Master/Guide at the back of each volume includes concise articles of historical interest, definitions of terms, and summaries of feature articles in the volume. Helpful cross-references appear throughout all volumes. On many pages you will find illustrations and descriptions of Project Plans and Home Plans, identified by the abbreviations PP and HP. For information on ordering these plans write to Good Decorating Plans Editor, Greystone Press, 225 Park Avenue South, New York, N.Y. 10003.

GATES

Use Them to Delimit Your Property And to Decorate It

The first impression of a home is often made right at the front gate. Unless the owner happens to be a misanthropic recluse, the gate should not be forbidding. It should be attractively designed so that it enhances both the appearance of the property behind it and the appearance of the street in general. A gate is, of course, a means of obtaining privacy and protection; but it can also be an object of charm when designed in a style suitable to the architecture of the house.

Privacy is becoming a major luxury in these days of too many people in too-small houses and apartments. Privacy is sought outdoors as well as in: pleasures like sunbathing, naps in a hammock, and breakfasts alfresco are more enjoyable when screened from the view of neighbors. Privacy means controlling as far as possible the outside scene framed from inside by the picture window, so that one does not look out to find others looking in.

Finally, privacy also means respecting the right of your neighbors to be shielded from unavoidable observance of your outdoor areas. Occasional backyard bacchanalia may be of interest to them; at other times, your privacy is their privacy.

Protection, as well as privacy, is provided by a gate, and the degree of protection required will have some influence on the kind of gate you choose. Gardeners want to keep stray dogs and roaming children away from newly seeded lawns or freshly planted flower beds, and for this you will need a gate that can be latched.

Whether needed for stringent protection or merely for added privacy, gates are more than just functional equipment. They are part of the architecture of your property, and should be in a style appropriate to your house and garden. An ornate wrought-iron gate is fine for a mansion, but a ranch house would call for something simpler—perhaps a roughhewn gate to match fencing in similar style.

Wood paneling and wire mesh are used in an unusual way in this gate and matching fence. Panels of 1-inch-square wire mesh alternate with 1x6 boards placed an inch apart to permit ventilation. The high wood panels provide adequate privacy, making the small court beyond secluded, and the pattern of the wire mesh adds a contemporary look.

Choosing style, material, color

Gates need not match the adjacent walls and fences; sometimes they can create a break—in color, height, material, or design—making a welcome change in a long fence line and indicating unmistakably the entrance to the home. A high, enclosing fence, perhaps of horizontal redwood panels, ensuring privacy while admitting air and light into a garden area, is a popular choice where a garden fronts a busy street or where neighbors seem too close.

A gate that is functional but breaks visually with the fence—one that admits light and air—

This gate of expanded metal, redwood strips, and painted plywood has varishaped rectangles arranged into a pleasing effect. Divided into nine spaces—each of different proportions and with three bright colors echoing the colors of the garden flowers—the gate admits light and permits free flow of air.

A low, single-story house in the Deep South appears cool and serene beyond an adobe-like wall that has a small gate of open construction. The fast-growing sky-flower vine with blooms of celestial blue softens the harsh glare of the sun on the stucco wall. Both gate and wall are designed in a traditional style often found in regions of hot climate.

may be constructed of colorful painted panels combined with expanded metal. This metal mesh is cut to size when it is purchased, and it should be spray-painted as the first step in assembling the gate. Paint the metal a color that closely matches the color of the fence; splashes of bright color can be added on the solid panels.

To hold metal and wood panels together, a narrow wood frame should be constructed. The metal mesh is then nailed in, and the wooden divider strips are added.

Cut the solid panels from scraps of exterior-grade plywood, fit them into the sections you have arranged with dividers, and nail them in place. For the best effect use these panels on both sides. Finally, seal or stain the wood frame and dividers, and paint the panels in colors that relate to the house or the garden.

In a wall that is solidly constructed of wood, stone, or concrete, a gate of light, open construction permits a tantalizing glimpse of garden and house beyond, and prevents a too-isolated appearance. Sometimes a gate of fanciful design makes a pleasing contrast to the long, flat surface of the wall; or the gate may be kept simple and unobtrusive, continuing

the line of the wall—high or low—with a flowering vine decorating the gatepost.

An open and shut case

A main factor that will influence your choice of gate will be the question of how careful you will need to be about keeping it closed. Some gates are designed more or less as decoration, with hardly a hint of "keep out" about them; others, more solidly constructed, are provided with sturdy latches and bolts—and though they may not have a warning sign on them, they can be unmistakably a barrier against intrusion.

Most likely you will want a gate that does not look as if it were part of the Berlin wall, but that does stay firmly closed in storms, and that will, when secured shut by bolt or simple hook, make a casual intruder think twice before opening it.

Whatever device you use to secure the gate, choose the hardware as carefully as you choose the gate itself.

Spoke gates with matching fence are old-time favorites. Here, the curved top rail makes this gate an eye-catcher. The top rail is actually two pieces cut from a 2 × 8-inch board and then fitted together and notched to receive the upright spokes. The post ornaments are shaped by milling at a lumber yard.

Use of ball and chain makes gate self-closing. Chain is attached to top of gate at a point slightly less than halfway across, and at bottom to adjacent post. Chain must be long enough so gate can open 90 degrees, high enough so that the concrete ball does not touch the ground.

This contemporary gate treatment suits many modern homes. Straight, simple lines make it an attractive addition to the garden. Frame and upright members are made of 2 × 4-inch redwood. Two 1½-inch dowels brace the gate through the center. The gate is treated with wood preservative.

A latch of black wrought iron fastens this gate of unfinished planking. The smooth-working thumb lever extends through the gate to lift the latch on the opposite side. For locking the gate from the inside, the latch slides, bolt-fashion, into the post or masonry so that it cannot be lifted from outside.

The same latch as above, viewed from the back of the gate. Note how the end of the thumb lever inserts under latch to raise it. This picture shows the latch in locked position—it has been slid to the left into the post by means of curved lever at right. Latch and hinges are easily installed.

Latches, locks, and lamps

Latch it. Lock it. Light it. Good advice to gatekeepers who want gates to provide safe and hospitable entry to family and friends, while protecting them against unwanted intruders or careless damage to prized gardens and plants from free-running dogs and other pets. Handsome wrought-iron latches and hinges, adaptations of Early American designs, are available in a variety of sizes. They are easy to attach, and visually they combine well with crude gates of unfinished planks and 2x4s. Since the latch, when set to lock, cannot be lifted from the front, it serves as an effective barrier to casual wanderers, youthful retrievers of lost baseballs, or just everyday seekers of shortcuts who menace flower beds and lawns.

The swinging garden gate that can be pushed in or out and that swings back to rest of its own momentum is a special benefit to the hurried, to the forgetful, and to those who simply will not bother to close the gate. Its unique hinge and pivot (the principle is the same as the swinging barroom door of Western-movie fame) will close the gate automatically. Allow room for the gate to swing freely in both directions.

Where space is limited, a wide gate can be divided into two sections joined by a latch. Double gate doors will be less likely to sag and will be easier to handle.

Where there is a long, unlighted path between the street and the house, gate lights are a practical as well as decorative addition. The glowing lamps will permit safe passage along the street and up to the front door. Gate lights will also be a protection against turned ankles and the accidents (most of which occur in your own backyard) that result from tripping over toys, garden hose, or poorly lit steps.

Outdoor lighting adds aesthetic interest along with safety. Trees and shrubs are dramatized, taking on a character totally different from their daytime look; and intricate shadows are cast across the lawn and against the side of the house. Fountains, pools, and brooks are especially beautiful when lit at night.

Mailboxes and house numbers are often integral parts of a gate complex, and when planning a fence and gate some time should be taken to choose an appropriate style and material for these items. When designing a mailbox, remember that the post office has regulations concerning the construction, size, and height of a unit. Beyond that, your imagination is free to create an object that will complement your property.

Gate swings inward and outward from a single point of suspension. Hardware consists of a brace for the top of the gate, a pivot bar, and two stirrup hinges and pins. Gate swings out and up, swings back automatically when released.

The white picket fence, simple and unpretentious, continues to be a traditional favorite. The flowering vine and large pots of roses make this gate especially appealing—an inviting entrance to a charming flagstone path.

Two gate lamps adorn this privacy screen and gate constructed from roughhewn boards. Fence framework is 4 × 4 posts with 2 × 4 crossmembers top and bottom. Posts are set either in concrete or about 3 feet deep into the ground.

Swinging on the garden gate is a time-honored joy of childhood so use heavy-duty hinges and indulge the youngsters. This small gate, on a path through the low hedge into the garden area, has a decorative panel made of 1½-inch wood dowels. Posts are treated with preservative.

An old gate of lacy iron grillwork is used here as a superb piece of decoration rather than as a functioning gate. It has been placed to screen a utility area at one side of the house and hung with pots of flowers in the Spanish patio style. The tendrils of the plants repeat the delicate pattern of the iron.

High and low

Gates that are very wide are usually awkward to handle; a fence or wall with an extra-wide opening is best equipped with a double gate. Gates can be impressively tall, however, without causing any problems—as long as they are supported on an adequate number of strong hinges. The height of the gate will generally be dictated by the height of the fence, but sometimes the house itself is designed so that a gate can fit between two of its walls to enclose a small entrance court, and here is where a tall, wrought-iron gate is quite effective.

A very low gate, on the other hand, would be appropriate when the opening is through a low hedge rather than a fence. Narrow, unobtrusive gateposts can be set at the hedge break, and a small gate hung to mark the way through.

Decorative indoor gates are made from stairway spindles. Make a framework of 1 × 2 pine (these frames are 18 inches wide). Mount plywood sheets in bottom sections, topped with another 1 × 2. Place a horizontal 1 × 2 to divide the space above in half, then nail spindles into the two open sections.

The homemade gate

A homemade gate can be designed and constructed by heeding a few simple rules. Choose a style of gate to harmonize with the architecture of your home. Consider color, finish, and, above all, the lines of the house. A practical gate should be at least 3 feet wide in order to accommodate deliveries of major appliances and the bulkiest furniture.

Sometimes you can save money by obtaining salvage or inexpensive lumber that, when dressed up with paint, will appear every bit as attractive as more expensive woods. However, do *not* take shortcuts when preparing the wood. Taking special care to cover the cut ends, paint or presoak it with a good chemical wood preservative. Ground moisture from below will quickly rot unprotected wood.

Follow the manufacturer's directions for using the preservative. Use it generously, and allow plenty of time for it to soak into the wood. The expense of money and time will be well repaid by a long life for your gate.

Before you attempt to hang the finished product, make sure the posts are set solidly in position—either into concrete or deep into the ground. If the weight of the unit calls for extra support, reinforce both the gate and the posts against sag and warping.

Redwood and most cedars are popular for gate construction because they are highly resistant to decay, but even these woods do not have the decay resistance of wood fully impregnated with an effective preservative. Redwood and most cedar needs special preservatives and are best left unpainted. The heartwood of the tree is the most durable part, the sapwood being more susceptible to decay. Heartwood of resistant species, however is increasingly difficult to obtain.

After the gate has been hung, the final task is painting it. Use one of the many tough exterior paints available, and coat the hardware to protect it from rust.

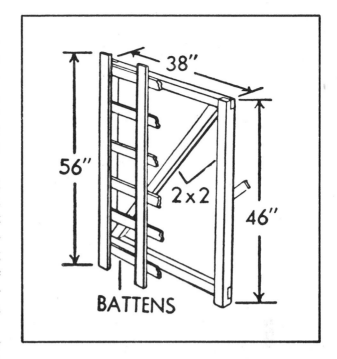

An easy-to-make gate of battens on a frame of 2 × 2s will fit a fence or hedge. As shown in the construction diagram, the gate dimensions are 38 inches by 56 inches. A Z-support braces the gate against sagging. Wood was presoaked in preservative to protect against rot.

Make a Nostalgic Outdoor Retreat Work for Your Modern Needs

Trying to define a gazebo is more a matter of defining what it isn't than what it is. It is *not* a tool shed, or a greenhouse, or a playhouse, although it may be playful. A gazebo does not have beds, although many a nap will be enjoyed there. If, when you look at the pictures here of gazebos, you immediately ask, "Yes, but what is it for," perhaps you need a gazebo to relax in.

For a gazebo is a structure for sitting in and gazing out of—that about sums up its uses. Its ancestry is ancient and universal; gazebos were built thousands of years ago and have been constructed in some form in almost every country. So, obviously, it has answered a real and continuing human need. In China, the gazebo was a spot for private meditation; in Japan, it symbolized the unity of man and nature. In Persia, it was a carpeted kiosk; in Spain it was called a *glorietta* and in Italy, it was a *belvedere*.

Modern gazebos

What is a gazebo now? It still varies in form, although most are built in circles, octagons, or squares, rather than rectangles, but it remains a structure devoted simply and lightheartedly to sitting. Always, there is a view to delight the eye—even if it is a view of a tiny tract-house garden. A gazebo can provide shelter from the sun or wind, and often it has built-in shelves or tables as well as seats, so that refreshments can be served to make watching the view even more pleasant. Its architecture can suit the owner's house or merely blend into the garden unobtrusively. As you can see from the photographs that accompany this article, there are infinite variations on the gazebo theme. Perhaps because the gazebo does not suit a serious

purpose (its shelter is often whimsical and imaginative, rather than solid), it often has a grace and charm that make it far more appealing than much more complicated structures.

There are some principles to keep in mind as you plan the construction of a gazebo. If you are going to build one close to your house, it should not clash with architecture of the main structure and should be made of the same materials, if possible.

Try to imagine how the gazebo will be used. You will probably want to read there, so it may be useful to have adjustable canopies or curtains to regulate the light.

Because it should relate to the outdoors, you may want to provide a climbing structure for roses or perhaps grape or wisteria vines. And, if you are terribly romantic, honeysuckle.

The dimensions may suit your needs, but keep in mind that you are not building a real house or playroom. Part of a gazebo's intimate charm is derived from small dimensions and a feeling that it is a cozy nook, separated from the rest of the world. If it can be opened up completely, it may then serve as a shelter for refreshment tables when you give a party, even though it is comparatively small in size.

The gazebo occupies a small space; the total floor area is 11 × 5 ½ feet. The flooring is made of 2 × 4s on edge and the floor frame is 1 × 6-inch boards. Two facing benches are 8½ feet long and are solidly made of 2 × 3s also on edge, resting on the aggregate piers. The roof support system is exposed, the components acting as decoration in a style reminiscent of Japanese tea houses. Wood shingles top the structure. Everything, including plastic-covered cushions, will shrug off rain, and weathering will only mellow the look of the gazebo which provides an outdoor haven for everyone in the family.

Relating the design to the main house

Naturally the design of the gazebo is as important to the garden's appearance as its placement. When a gazebo is close to the main house, the two should be architecturally related. Perhaps the gazebo can repeat the shape of the larger building. Certainly it can be built of the same material, whether it is wood or masonry.

On the other hand, if your home is made of brick, with wooden shutters, a wooden gazebo

This rustic gazebo, blending so perfectly with the wooded property on which it was built, would harmonize with almost any style house because it seems a part of the setting. Its wood elements show off their natural beauty, and its aggregate concrete piers repeat the stones and pebbles of the pathway that leads to the gazebo.

A gazebo in a garden corner, above, is close to the house and therefore the wood of its posts, beams and roof is stained to match the siding of the house and the fence close by. The base is a 4-inch-thick circle of concrete 18 feet in diameter. Posts are 2x4s, beams are 2x8s and the strips of the roof are 1x2s. A canvas cover that fits the top provides shelter.

in the same color as the shutters would be equally compatible.

Sometimes the garden house is made from material used as a decorative element on the main building, such as lacy ironwork or Victorian fretwork. Always, when the gazebo is close to the house, the same degree of formality or informality is maintained.

You can build in as much privacy as you want. The structure can be closed, with a door or canvas curtains enclosing the inside, or the gazebo can be an open structure that merely gives the feeling of a little house.

Relating the gazebo to nature

Depending on its placement, a gazebo can close a space, terminate a path, provide privacy, dramatize a corner of the garden or a stretch

An airy confection suggestive of soft summer twilight and lovers' trysts, this enchanting gazebo was designed around an antique spiral staircase and a wire-mesh aviary reminiscent of a type popular during the Italian Renaissance. Despite its apparent fragility, the gazebo has a sturdy steel framework, whose uprights are sunk deep into a concrete base. Rounded arches and quatrefoil design in the frame and the birdcage give the gazebo something of a medieval flavor. A romantic addition to the gazebo might be night lights (bug repellent, of course) to cast a twinkling glow over the garden and the trees beyond. What visitor could resist the temptation to climb to the gazebo's top and enjoy the spectacle of setting sun or rising moon, or better yet, declaim a few lines from *Romeo and Juliet* to the accompaniment of a nightingale.

Punctuating a pool terrace, above, is an umbrella-topped gazebo. Three sides are closed for privacy and protection from the wind. At poolside parties after dark, the structure becomes a bar lighted from the peak; during the day bathers can sun here out of the path of strong breezes. Although the walls are simple, the rafters are beautifully carved. Potted plants and tiki lights add a festive note.

of wall, emphasize an artful group of plantings, or complement the main house.

If the property is large and the gardens extensive, the gazebo may be built at a distance from the house itself. This means its appearance can differ greatly from the style of the house. The relationship to seek then is to the garden or landscape—to nature. The setting, if dense and thicketlike, calls for a rather rustic building. Its materials can make it part of nature: log walls perhaps, a thatched roof in some areas of the country, siding finished in either bark colors or a leafy hue. In a stark setting, a starkly designed gazebo looks right: for example, walls of stone are effective where natural stones form the dominant feature of the terrain; weathered siding, echoing the look of bleached driftwood, is appropriate for a gazebo close to the sea.

How to Design a Pretty Room For Little Girls to Grow Up In

Sugar and spice—or anything else that's nice—can be the mood-setting motif that meets the needs and tastes of a girl with a room of her own. A garden of colors transplanted indoors brings to a girl's room a ruffled and delicate bouquet, an arrangement of potted leafy ferns, and fields of flowers printed on wallpaper and fabrics. The blossom-printed fabrics, the cob-web-fine curtains create a room that is a soft setting for romantic daydreaming or enchanted evenings. A deep pink area rug, matched with the tall, painted armoire, adds a strong color note against which the wallpaper and bedspread are played. The petal-pink cushion on the bed blends prettily with the daffodil-yellow cushion beside it. More garden colors are the daffodil yellow of the painted chest, and the fern-green chair cushion.

Imagine a girl's room that is dynamic and vital in mood—decorated in vibrant colors, exciting reds and yellows flashing brilliantly against a jungle-green background. This room provides shelves with ample space for books and treasured souvenirs. A handsome tailored cover helps make the daybed a daytime conversation corner that converts at night to sleeping space. In this room, wallpaper and matching fabric, covering wall, ceiling, and window shades with one unbroken patterned area, provide a strong background for the yellow-covered daybed. The red from the wallpaper pattern is repeated in the ceiling cornice above the bed and the green of the wallpaper is seen again on the bookcase wall. The entire scheme is inexpensive and easy to do. But above all a girl's room should be a haven—a place for living, sleeping, and working.

Now you see them, now you don't—so cleverly have the long narrow windows on the wall above the bed been integrated into the canopy design. First, cut the ceiling-mounted scalloped cornice from an 8-foot, 1 × 6 board. Paint the edging and wood corner braces jungle-plumage colors—brilliant reds, yellows, and greens. Mount the ceiling cornice to align with the outer edge of the bed. Paint window trim to match the color chosen for the bookcase wall. Apply wallpaper to wall and ceiling in the canopy area, and laminate matching fabric to window shades to complete the effect.

Soft summer breezes seem to be wafting through the garden-▶ fresh atmosphere of this delicately feminine room, gently stirring the gossamer curtains and graceful ferns. Flower-strewn wallpaper and the matching bedspread and bolster add a bouquet-like note of color, echoing the yellow chest and fern-green cushion. All are subtly lit by recessed ceiling lights and a wall-mounted globe fixture. For accent—the one perfect accessory, a leaf-green, leaf-shaped Tiffany-type pendant lamp. Behind the bedroom area is a simply furnished dressing room, which, with the addition of a desk lamp and bookcases, could easily be converted for use as a study.

Two strong patterns coexist harmoniously in this room. The secret of their compatibility is color. Bold pinks and greens are combined on the desk wall in an exciting plaid pattern; in the bed alcove, they appear in a geometric arrangement of diamonds and related figures. Bright patterns such as these have great visual impact, so use them sparingly to showcase one piece of furniture, or define one area of a room. To further neutralize the strong patterns used in this room, large amounts of solid pinks and greens, as well as cooling expanses of white, have been used in the scheme.

Define areas within the room

Sleeping, studying, dressing, and dreaming— these are just a few of the ways a girl spends her time in a room of her own. The study and sleep areas in one room can be dramatically differentiated with two bold patterns: plaid wallpaper to back up the white desk (where rests—though not often—a phone of her own); and a wallpaper of geometric shapes to delineate the built-in sleeping alcove, which is surmounted with medallion-like plaques. Color coordination is the key to the compatibility of the two patterns. The under-bed space is used efficiently for storing sweaters and other items.

Just for sleeping: hearts and flowers can be charmingly combined in a pink-and-white scheme with a fan-shaped wicker headboard beneath a regal canopy. The white accents are flattering, young and sweet—without a touch of the extreme that might make the mood cloying. For dressing: an old chest and mirror tie into the scheme via an inexpensive decorating trick of making the mirror match the curtains. A small amount of coordination results in a highly successful decorative effect.

Carnation-printed bed sheets and a canopy create a royal setting for sleeping. A 1 × 2 wood support with a fluorescent fixture attached is fastened with toggle bolts to the wall at the correct height for the canopy. The canopy top is crafted of ¼-inch plywood. To sew the hangings, first make a gathered valance, then cut a double sheet in half for the side panels. Hand-stitch the side panels to the valance and staple both to the back of the canopy top. The full dust ruffle is made from additional sheets.

Make a match of the mirror and window on the same wall with floral-printed fabric. A snip of extra curtain fabric glued onto the mirror frame makes the magic. Chest fronts are painted a rosy hue to match the rug and accent the red flowers in the curtain print. Lavender velveteen cushions the white wicker chair and footstool near the window. There is more white on the tops of the chests and in the lamp and the drawer pulls.

Black looks more striking when it is used sparingly and is poised against white or cream-colored walls. Here, the black note is a mirror frame, like an exclamation point above the ivory-finished chests of drawers and bookshelves that line the wall. Note how the shape of the corner window is repeated by the corner desk beneath it and accented by the black desk chair. Pattern interest is provided by the red roses floating freely over the ceiling and down the wall behind the bed. A rich, red bedspread provides a solid block of color interest.

A very big decorating drama is played on a tiny stage in this scheme for a small space. Starring role is played by the tall, turned bedposts that form the headboard. Wall-to-wall carpeting in soft green has a spacious effect; and while one green wall echoes the carpet, the remaining walls are white to enlarge the enclosure visually. The room has a serene air which is created partially through the use of cool, low-key colors—lush blues and greens repeated in the figured bedspread, the carpet, the walls, tall louvered doors, pillows, even in one of the tiny night tables by the bed. Another factor contributing to the room's serenity is its lack of clutter. No strong patterns have been used. The furniture is functional and slim, not bulky, and it is used sparsely. There are only a few accessories and they are simple—airy ferns and an elegant hanging lamp.

The misty impressionist painting hung at eye level near the desk keys this period room setting in ivory and old rose tones. Flower-printed, ribbon-striped pink and green window shades and floor-length draperies are rich and warming beneath flower-embellished cornices. Desk, at right angles to the wall, has a prized collection of porcelain figurines and animals ranged on shelves above. The rose-colored rug and ivory walls contribute to the muted mood of a hand-painted miniature. A comfortable armchair covered in rose-colored fabric is elegant enough for a living room, but not out of place in this formal bedroom. The ivory desk chair is similarly elegant, but light enough in scale to combine well with the desk. The entire room scheme is traditional, ladylike, old-world in feeling.

Striking accents enhance the room

Room accents can be as strong as punctuation marks, decisively calling attention to themselves, contrasting boldly with the room decor as in this black-accented bedroom. Modular furniture units are arranged along the length of one wall and hold a variety of secondary accessories—a cheerleader's megaphone, the breadboard display of miniature copper cooking pots, the papier-mâché head holding magazines. But the center of attention is the black-framed mirror, and, closely seconding it, the black chair.

Pictures and paintings with complete color palettes of their own can be translated successfully into room color schemes. Here, an impressionist painting is the starting point for a traditionally formal ivory and old rose room scheme, although it remains an unobtrusive element in the room as a whole. In the small blue-green room, the tall, turned, and twisted bed-

posts are an eye-catching accent, bringing the eye upward, as do the rattan valet chair and the hanging light fixture, and resulting in a feeling of spaciousness.

Girls' rooms that grow up

A little bit of forethought in planning room schemes pays big dividends. You can save time, effort, and money by remembering that as your daughter grows, her tastes and enthusiasms will change. However, no matter what her age, some of her needs remain constant. A place to sleep, a place to store clothes, a place to do schoolwork are always necessary. When buying beds, floor coverings, chests, and chairs, think of them as long-term investments. These expensive purchases, carefully chosen, act as a nucleus that can be renewed again and again to meet their owner's needs whatever age or stage. Look for well-constructed furnishings that will withstand the wear and tear of childhood years and can be rejuvenated later to go with fresh paint, new wallpaper, and bedspreads. From the start, provide adequate storage for clothing, books, hobbies, and knickknacks—adequate storage space encourages neatness. (And "A place for everything and everything in its place" minimizes the proverbial teen-age messiness as well.)

Do not forget good lighting—it is a "must" whether she is studying home economics or experimenting with cosmetics. If you have been careful in choosing floor coverings and furnishings, you can be carefree with accessories. Rely on pictures, toys, posters, hobby collections—whatever is your daughter's fancy at the moment—to re-do a room inexpensively. A re-painting of old chests or beds, and a new set of curtains and bedspreads can transform a tomboy's lair into a debutante's delight. Sometimes, even the unlikeliest of items bridges the gap from babyhood to childhood and can be reused in a fresh imaginative way—witness the bassinet now doing as a catchall for a collection of stuffed animals. Part of the fun of redecorating is choosing the colors and doing the sewing or painting, so let your daughter participate in the refurbishing—she'll enjoy the room more when it's finished.

Rooms for young ladies

Almost old enough to be on her own? Here is a girl's room designed to span the years from

A monochromatic color scheme brightens a dark room and is space-enhancing in a small one. Here cool, serene greens, ranging from light yellow-green to chartreuse and lime green, are accented with white. The green plaid wallpaper is used imaginatively on the ceiling and sawtooths down onto the wall for a tent-like effect.

late teens to over-21. Blue-green walls and carpeting create a one-color shell that intensifies the brilliance and impact of yellow furniture and the yellow and white printed fabric. To set off the window recess, the wall is draped with daisy-printed fabric, a bright note of gaiety that is repeated in the bedspread.

Stained wood shutters with louvers allow for maximum control of light; they can be folded back to let the sunlight flood in, or be adjusted for partial light and privacy. Chest-and-shelf units flank a matching yellow desk-dressing table, reiterating the yellow headboard and end table. The yellow of the lamp and of the chair upholstery restate the yellow theme. The tailored lines of the furniture—with just a hint of the Orient in the bamboo motif—were simple enough for a child's room, and now,

Blue-green walls and carpeting blend together quietly, making a calm background against which the sunshine-yellow furniture and cheery yellow and white daisy-printed fabrics glow. One-color shell intensifies the warm tones of the painted furniture, dramatizes the oversized daisy print.

rearranged and repainted, serve handsomely in the more sophisticated setting. The classic Chinese shapes of the ceramic lamps emphasize the Oriental motif. Other add-on pieces to complete the transformation from a youngster's room to a young lady's domain include the chair-side wicker table and the bench in front of the dressing table. In both pieces the green end of the blue-green spectrum is picked up. This subtle change from the dominant blue brings richness and depth to the color palette

Accessories and color make one mood in this bedroom with connected bath. A contemporary lavatory-vanity combination in the bathroom is enhanced by a spindle-back chair, wood mirror frame, and floor-standing towel rack, old-time accents that blend well with the modern fixtures. Lending a Victorian touch is the framed daguerreotype on the bedroom wall. Window shutters are easy-to-keep and also recall an earlier time. Repeating the gold of the bathroom walls, floor, and vanity is the antique gold of the bedspread. Pale green bedroom walls meet the deeper green of the wall-to-wall carpeting and the bed's tailored, box-pleated dust ruffle. Green towels in the bath are another color coordinating accessory in a green and gold scheme that successfully ties together the two rooms.

◄ Shades of rosy red and soft yellow unify and define an odd-shaped attic containing all the essentials for a girl's room. A floral pattern combining both colors is used for the bedspread and covers the area behind the bed, forming a mock headboard. The same floral print was applied to the ceiling and covers the cushions of the built-in window seat. A glowing yellow warms the wide, bare floorboards and forms the curlicue design on the area rug. The warm red accentuates the shuttered gables, making a strong decorating point of the attic's architectural features. A shade of mossy green was chosen for the wicker chairs. Turquoise chair cushions are cool accents for the room. The wicker chairs and table were about-to-be-discarded porch furniture when they were rescued and made usable again by a coat of fresh paint and new cushions.

of the room without adding a new and distracting color note. A softening touch to the room scheme is the minimal bed canopy—skinny side-curtains are graceful without being stifling.

An attic provides extra space

This under-the-eaves hideaway, tucked under the roof so tightly that you can almost hear rain drumming above, was once a dusty attic space, abandoned and unused. Now, all its homey, homely nooks and crannies delightfully underscored by the unconventional use of color, it has been transformed into a girl's room with its unique, old-fashioned country charm preserved for a new generation. The odd shape of the room is defined and unified by the use of two basic colors: strong, shocking pink and soft orange. Bright pink accentuates the gabled windows, which are closed by shutters. Window seats (wonderful for rainy-day reading) and drawer storage are built in snugly underneath. The old, wide-board floor, a rare and genuine "country" touch, is painted a soft orange. Vertical siding—part of the still-surviving original attic—is painted white. The sprightly floral pattern used for the bedspread, the panel behind the bed, the ceiling, and the cushion on the window seat combines both shocking pink and soft orange, uniting the pink and orange colors used elsewhere in the room. Beneath the bed, a white area rug picks up and repeats the soft orange in its curlicue design. Mossy green painted wicker chairs and turquoise chair cushions are cool accents for the room and repeat a color from the bedspread fabric.

Accessories effectively recall the mood of bygone days in this very modern bath. Echoes of the early American colonial period are the period chair, wood mirror frame, and floor-standing tower rack. Shuttered windows and the framed daguerreotype on the wall in the adjoining bedroom hearken back to earlier times too. Linking bedroom to bathroom is the green and yellow color scheme.

GLASS WALL TREATMENTS

A View of the Great Outdoors Can Be Cannily Engineered

The general trend in modern twentieth-century decorating is to create an indoor setting that is enhanced by the natural beauty of the surrounding landscape. Now that heating and cooling are no longer a problem, glass walls, large picture windows, sliding glass doors, and contrasting clear, translucent, and opaque multi-paneled house sidings provide a whole new facet in house transformation.

Renovate with glass

The modern householder discovers that the crisp crystal whiteness of a snowy day or the sharp cutting shadows of blazing summer sun as seen through glass walls can add dimension and excitement to the decor of his house, whatever the period setting may be. The ef-

fectiveness of the heating or air conditioning will not be seriously diminished.

The traditionally low-ceilinged, small-windowed New England house or the Victorian nook-and-crannied multiroomed home were constructed to retain heat because the longest period of the year was cold. Now modern heating and insulation provide the necessary heat retention, and remodeling in many older buildings can be done with an eye for light and view. Glass provides the ideal material.

Frequently, dark hallways are successfully transformed into bright entrances by inserting glass wall panels alongside and above a front door facing a staircase. The glass allows light to brighten a large area and at the same time gives a panoramic view.

This lovely new indoor-outdoor family room was charmingly transformed from a summer patio by using glass walls and a mansard roof. It is a perfect gathering place for enjoying a summer garden or a wintry Christmas morning. The sliding storm doors help keep the winter winds out, and the old-style ceiling fans start the breeze circulating on a sultry night.

Effective screening by surrounding woodlands provides the living room with privacy and serenity. Carefully placed outdoor lighting prevents large mirrorlike reflections on the glass walls at night and adds a touch of cool green from outdoors to complement the warm melon and rust tones. The living room and dining room, forming one large room with glass walls on three sides, are separated by the fireplace.

The roughhewn stone wall, serving as a backdrop for the buffet in the dining room and the green of the heavily wooded area outdoors, accents the delicacy of both Japanese and Chinese accessories. The glass walls of this room make it possible for the beauty indoors and outdoors to be enjoyed at the same time. The vast expanse of open wall makes it possible to have longer hours of warm natural light.

This entryway is bathed in light coming through the attractive wood-beamed glass wall that frames the front door. During daylight hours the flow of light creates a feeling of open space and makes the garden a part of the house. The two-story window wall also enlarges the entry hall to form a perfect anteroom for dinner party guests.

A summer patio or porch can become an all-year-round gathering place for family and friends with the addition of glass walls. Yet the enjoyment of the outdoor scene is extended when the climate can be controlled. This room becomes the perfect spot for informal outdoor dining in warm weather, or a charming addition to the living room and dining room for cocktails before dinner any time of the year. If the floor of the former patio is tile, terrazzo, or slate, a small rug or throw rugs would be a warm touch.

Many older beach houses were built with small windows as protection from high winds, with a small door leading to a porch, sundeck, or walkway. The interior was often dark and gloomy in contrast to the pleasant sunny scene and the unlimited ocean view outside. That can all be changed now with sliding glass doors installed in a dining alcove, a master bedroom, or in the living-dining room. Sliding glass doors are particularly suitable for the beach scene or damp climates, if they are tempered safety-glass, or thermopaned for storm door protection. They should be set in aluminum or steel frames to protect against warping.

Types of glass

Glass has many natural advantages, and new developments in appearance and in strength have made it a major building material. Thermopane is another name for custom-designed climate. It helps retain heat in winter and keeps the cold out. It does an equally efficient job in summer by keeping heat out and air conditioning in. Glass also comes in special strengths so that if a glass wall is located in a spot where an occasional ball might find its mark, properly tempered glass will remain unscarred. Tinted glass shades an overly bright location, in the south or west, and cuts glare.

In modern architecture, glass enclosures are often designed to take advantage of heating that cuts fuel bills. Combine this with the endless possibilities of using the outdoor view as an actual part of the interior decor, and suddenly, with appropriate landscape design, there is a wide-open feeling of space and privacy.

Translucent glass makes a wonderfully easy wall to maintain in a bathroom, yet lets in light while providing as much privacy as any masonry wall. The glassed area can be much larger than the ordinary bathroom window.

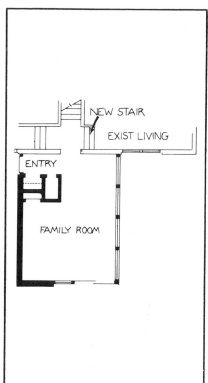

When this family built a new addition to their house they chose the new, modern look that glass gives. Glass walls, such as the ones in the picture above, give an open, contemporary feeling to any house. But the addition was practical too. As shown in the diagram, the addition provided not only a new rear entryway, but also a new closet, ideal for storing garden tools or outdoor tablecloths. The new room expands living space and gives the family a cheerful gathering place.

The large glass walls let in the sunshine and greenery of the outdoors, adding a feeling of spaciousness to this contemporary family room. The glass doors at the end of the room provide easy access to the garden and can be opened in warmer weather. Notice the draperies at the far end of the room. These can be drawn for privacy, or, as shown in the picture, they can be left open to let the outdoors in. The bright outdoor scenery adds color to the monochrome room.

Know the Shapes of Glasses Appropriate to Every Drink

"Fill ev'ry glass, for wine inspires us, and fires us with courage, love, and joy." Not that glasses are not used for other things, some less inspiring than wine. No matter what nourishing or convivial liquid fills the glass, it always looks and tastes better in a pretty one. When setting the table for family or friends, do not underestimate the important effect glassware can create. A bright red or blue goblet can change the whole feeling of a table setting. An elegant champagne glass adds a touch of ceremony and formality; a pressed glass goblet denotes a casual, informal occasion. Glassware plays just as important a role in table fashion as silver, china, linens, and flowers. And just as a simple hamburger is much more appealing on a colorful pottery plate than on a plain white paper one, so a glass of vin ordinaire gains importance in a graceful stemmed goblet.

Glass consists of sand plus various bases. These include potash, lime, or lead oxide. Crystal is an especially durable form of glass noted for its brilliance and clear bell-like ring when struck. Crystal is made of flint and lead oxide. Ordinary glass contains no lead and therefore has no ring and little sparkle by comparison. Cut glass is crystal that has been cut in faceted patterns that reflect light and add highlights and brilliance. Pressed glass, made famous in Sandwich, Massachusetts, is made by pouring molten glass into molds, where it is pressed into patterns. Pressed glass is made in a variety of colors and is usually used with informal table settings. Hand-blown and pressed, or molded, glass are both produced today, and each variety is valuable for its particular purpose. Hand-blown crystal is precious, expensive, and breakable and is therefore usually not used every day.

A brief history

The history of crystal is rich with examples of elaborately decorated hand-blown glass. Perhaps the best known comes from Venice,

This breakfast table is set with rosy linen mats to echo the bright red of the wall. The tole flower container holds baby roses, continuing the color scheme. Pale green cereal bowls blend with the painted ladder-back chairs and the greenery of the centerpiece. The tall cranberry goblets give this setting an extra dimension. Stemmed glassware such as this always looks more important than tumblers.

The holiday dinner table successfully combines the use of two strong colors for a dramatic effect. Two fuchsia sari silk scarves drape the sides of the table while the center is left bare to reveal the gleaming wood. Three groups of American Beauty roses are banked in greens and interspersed with candles to provide a centerpiece. The startling accent of Bristol blue goblets and soup bowls makes this table particularly effective. Bristol is a famous English glass product.

which has been famous for its glass production since the Middle Ages. Venetian glass is well known for its ornamental and exceptionally light and delicate qualities. Much of it was enameled and gilded in pictorial or abstract patterns.

Some of the other famous glass-producing areas of the world are Ireland, where Waterford glass originated; England, famous for Bristol glass, and France, where Lalique is now being manufactured. Beautiful cased glass was produced in Bohemia, and Sweden boasts many fine crystal factories, among them Orrefors. America is the home of Sandwich glass and the incomparable Louis C. Tiffany works, as well as many present-day manufacturers of every kind of glassware from heavy lead crystal to colorful pressed glass.

How to buy

When buying glassware, avoid the urge to buy matched sets of everything. First, think of the glasses used most frequently. Do you entertain a lot or not very often? Do you serve wine or beer frequently, or are you iced tea-totallers? Do you have a horde of milk-drinking children? When these and similar questions have been answered, start out by purchasing only those sizes used most often and add different shapes as the need arises. Remember to add some color to the glassware collection. An average wardrobe of glassware should include a dozen of each of the following: all-purpose glasses, wine glasses, goblets, glasses for highballs, and for the children, inexpensive tumblers. The illustrations used in this article include nearly every shape and size

An Oriental mood is imparted by the rather cool simplicity of this setting. The only softening touch is the delicate flower arrangement that adds necessary warmth to the otherwise stark table setting. The china is cool white with an encrusted black border. The black is picked up by the napkin and the geometric place mat, which has been fashioned from angularly cut vinyl tiles. The flatware has clean, functional lines. The real drama of this setting lies in the unusual glassware. The goblet is coal black and the wine glass has a clear bowl and stem on a black foot. Notice how the pink linen tablecloth also serves as a warm background for this setting, which looks almost like a still-life painting.

This formal Sunday luncheon table has been set in a traditional mood. The dining room, with its fireplace and Chippendale furniture, has an eighteenth-century feeling. In keeping with this style is the elegant yet simple white bone china with a scalloped gold border. The place mats also carry out the gold-on-white motif. The centerpiece of white and burnt-orange chrysanthemums picks up the theme. The beautiful lead crystal goblets are cut in a diamond pattern. The only other accessories on the table are all crystal, adding another note of formality. The covered butter dish and the footed compote, here used for preserves, are antiques. The ashtrays and salt cellars are also cut crystal.

A casual supper setting makes use of melamine dinnerware and a molded plastic tumbler. Plastic, one of today's most convenience-oriented products, is used everywhere in the modern home. One of the greatest attributes of plastic is that it comes in myriad colors, so that it can serve as a vibrant accent on a table while still being an inexpensive and practical purchase. It is a must with children.

This informal tabletop makes use of very few accessories yet is still an inviting setting. The circular place mat with its hemstitched border is a subtle background for the colorful everyday china. The amber pressed-glass tumbler picks up the warm tones in the china and the linen napkin. The stainless steel flatware is a reproduction of an old Queen Anne pattern — a three-tined fork and pistol-handled knife.

Breakfast becomes an inviting meal with this colorful setting. The stark white china has a delicate abstract border design, which is repeated in the Pennsylvania Dutch linen mat and napkin. A small arrangement of roses makes this a special breakfast indeed. The imaginative use of flowers is one of the many ways to make a setting memorable. For instance, had this been a breakfast tray, a single rose in a bud vase would have been effective. Here, an old-fashioned glass with a platinum band around the top awaits freshly squeezed orange juice. The ashtray is a polished shell.

Happy Thanksgiving! This festive family dinner table is typi- ▶ cal of many American Thanksgivings. The well-browned turkey, tossed green salad, and green beans hint at more traditional treats to come. Here, the table was set with a loosely woven, lettuce-green tablecloth and matching napkins. The bright yellow chrysanthemums reflect the glow of the candles, and the formal gold and white china invites everyone to a happy feast. The large tulip-shaped crystal water goblets are decorated with etched vertical lines that accent their long stems and give them an imposing stature. The crystal candle holders have faceted prisms to reflect the candlelight and make the whole table sparkle. A tall cut-glass decanter between the candles holds brandy.

of glass available. There are countless shapes and sizes of glassware—many more than one family would normally desire or have the space to store. However, many standard glass shapes can be used for other purposes. Just use a little imagination and transform a champagne goblet into a footed dessert dish for mousses, sherbets, or fruit. Grandmother's fingerbowls can be taken out of the attic and used for cold soups or desserts or, for a charming floral arrangement, float a few single blossoms in a fingerbowl of water.

Brown is beautiful in this monochromatic table setting. Everything from the raffia place mat to the autumn flowers echoes the same gold and brown tones. The china has a mottled two-toned look that adds warmth to the setting. The wooden-handled stainless steel flatware is well designed and very contemporary. The amber goblet has a lovely flared shape.

The shape is the thing in this luncheon setting. An octagonally shaped plate with a blue floral border sits on a circular navy blue place mat. The clear crystal goblet and wine glass have a tulip-shaped bowl with a flared lip. The napkin is folded in a neat rectangle, and the vertical lines of flower arrangement carry out this theme of line and shape.

The drama of black and gold is fitting for this after-the-theater supper setting. A black vinyl tray holds the gold- and black-bordered china and a black linen napkin trimmed with gold braid. A classic wine glass complements the setting with its gold-bordered rim. The exotic flower with its shiny dark leaves sits in a black-lacquered cigarette holder.

The glasses shown here, varied in size, shape, and style, represent just about every purpose to which a glass is put. Top row, from left to right: A chalice-shaped wine or water goblet, followed by an elaborately cut crystal wine glass. Next is a classic pressed-glass water goblet, often found in amber or ruby glass. Last is a formal crystal goblet decorated with an etched gold band at the top.

Middle row: Two contemporary Old Fashioned glasses, the first known as a double Old Fashioned. These, of course, have many other uses besides serving cocktails. In the middle is a champagne goblet, which can also serve as a sherbet or fruit dessert dish. The next are two after-dinner, or cordial, glasses. The first is a delicate cut-crystal glass, the second a large brandy snifter. While used usually as a drinking glass for brandy, a snifter can be effective as a bowl for floating flower blossoms—an attractive centerpiece.

Bottom row: A heavy Swedish wine glass with a distinctly modern shape is followed by a typical pilsner glass. The pilsner could also be used for serving parfaits or other iced desserts. Third is a highball glass, which is probably the most all-purpose glass in any house. Last is a wine glass in the familiar and beautifully simple tulip shape.

If Gardening Is Your Hobby, Indulge It Year-Round

The idea of using glass to enclose small gardens is relatively new, since it was not until the end of the nineteenth century that glass began to be produced at a reasonable price in large volume. However, glasshouses, another term for greenhouses, were in existence in the nineteenth century; and even before 1870, glasshouses had been built—usually as luxuries for the rich.

The practice of enclosing gardens dates back as far as the Fourth Dynasty in Egypt where interior courtyards in palaces were used as garden sites. The Greeks, too, had indoor palace gardens in the Mycenaean age. Although the gardens were not glass-enclosed, they could be considered the forerunners of our present-day glasshouses.

As the art of flower growing spread from southern Europe and Asia Minor to colder climates, cultivation had to be brought indoors. However, it was not until after World War I that private greenhouses became really popular in America. One result of the general prosperity at this time was a tremendous increase in greenhouses. Easy climate control is especially important for flower growing in the northern states and greenhouses were the ideal solution.

Greenhouses for the home

Indoor flower growing comes down to us as a time-honored art and pastime that can beautify both gardens and homes all year round. Greenhouses are an avid gardener's best friend.

Because temperature and humidity can be controlled in a greenhouse, many sorts of flowers can be grown. Tropical plants flourish in cold climates when indoor weather can be easily regulated by heating units and humidifiers.

Greenhouses need not be used only for tropical flowers that require special hothouse protection. Flowers that do well in the growing season in temperate climates can have a season that lasts year round. Carnations, chrysanthemums, snapdragons, and roses are among the flowers that thrive indoors as well as out.

In the more exotic range, orchids and gardenias, once considered aristocrats in the world of flowers, can now be raised quite easily in home greenhouses with proper weather controls. The more adventurous home gardener might want to try raising tomatoes, cucumbers, lemons, and oranges in his greenhouse.

Traditionally, greenhouses are thought of as structures separate from the house. Most are, but where there is not enough outdoor space for a greenhouse, plants can be raised in conservatories. These are actually part of a room. If the homeowner does have space for a greenhouse, it can be easily and cheaply constructed. Kits are available for the do-it-yourself builder.

Plastic greenhouses

New developments in plastic manufacturing make some heavy-duty plastics perfect building materials. Plastic does not shatter easily and it is strong. Yet it is quite flexible, a good deal

This packaged greenhouse came with full instructions for building at home. Plastic webbing on the sloping glass ceiling provides protection from too much sun. Electric devices at the top open part of the roof automatically when the temperature reaches a certain point. Control panels on wall at left are for adjusting temperature and humidity.

This simply constructed plant room, designed to be an integral part of the house, has a U-shaped bench of plants in pots sitting in gravel in metal liner trays. Water, just below bottom of pots, builds up essential humidity. Shade-tolerant plants (ferns, bromeliads) grow well under the bench. Roof of windows is chicken-wire glass—strong enough to resist snow.

Exterior view of do-it-yourself greenhouse shown on previous page. The 8-foot addition was built off the breakfast area, which had a 7-foot opening for a picture window. Old bricks were used for the foundation to harmonize with the house. Overhanging tree limb helps provide shade needed by the more fragile plants, such as gloxinias.

lighter than glass, and is easy to cut. Plexiglas can be cut with a home power saw; and Plio-film, which is much thinner, can be cut with a razor or sharp scissors. These plastics can then be tacked to a wooden frame or aluminum stripping.

Glass, however, has certain advantages over plastic. Unless shattered, it lasts longer and does not scratch as easily. With a greenhouse, whether of glass or plastic, favorite flowers continue to thrive no matter what the outside thermometer says.

The plant room pictured at top left is seen here from the outside. Herbs flourish outdoors, handy to the kitchen. They are grown in sections of flue tile, glimpsed at bottom right. The exposure of this room is east (preferred, with south next) so the intensity of light does not demand shading paint on the glass. This small addition transforms whole room.

A backyard has been constructed into a multilevel arrangement that includes an 11 × 13-foot greenhouse assembled from a kit. Included is automatic device for opening the top section of the roof when temperature goes too high. The lower level patio, directly outside the greenhouse door, is constructed of aggregate-concrete modules separated by 2 × 4s. The wooden deck at right is 8½ × 11½ feet, made with 2 × 4s nailed to 2 × 8-inch headers.

How to Pamper Your Guests In Niche, Corner, or Elegant Room

Hospitality is an art—and one with a history as old as civilization. Through the centuries, hospitality has been bestowed in thousands of different ways by hosts in as many different cultures. Today there are still endless variations on the art of making a guest welcome, but the essentials are the same everywhere, amongst all peoples; if the visitor finds a solicitous host or hostess, a comfortable bed, a reasonable degree of privacy, and palatable food, he feels he is truly welcome.

Today's guest room, sumptuous or modest, is part of this long tradition. In bygone days, when traveling called for even greater endurance than is now demanded by airports and bus terminals, the weary traveler might have found rest on a pallet by the fire or in a canopied bed in a palace. Guest accommodations are somewhat more standardized today, but even here in America there are interesting variations.

The separate guest house

The ultimate luxury for the guest is a small house completely separate from the main one, where he can stay up as late and sleep as long as he pleases, without fear of disrupting normal family routine. Such a house is not always as far beyond possibility as it may seem. Sometimes a room or two can be added above a garage, or the garage itself can be converted; or perhaps a garden shed will be large enough and sturdy enough to make remodeling worthwhile. Construction like this, of course, takes a fair amount of money, but will add greatly to the host's popularity—and to the value of his property.

Use space creatively

A separate guest house, however, is an indulgence not many of us can afford. In most urban and suburban areas there is an increasing demand for elbow room—which has been defined by one urban planner with a sense of humor leavening his sense of desperation as "enough room to swing a cat in—literally." If you have that, you are not too crowded.

Nowadays, using space creatively has become a necessity as well as an art. In a recent Broadway play the hero had a platform reached by a ladder in his one-room flat, and on it he kept a bed, bureau, and a friendly visitor. In New York's Greenwich Village, where there are still plenty of old houses with high rooms, such platforms are in great demand for extra sleeping quarters. If you have high-ceilinged rooms, you might add such a device to a den, a basement game room, or even to one corner of the living room—with the space underneath becoming a secluded retreat where floor pillows and a low table would be adequate furnishings.

Between the elegance of a separate guest house and the bohemianism of a sleeping platform there are a multitude of more ordinary arrangements for overnight guests. In the older

Shades of red bring a glow to this paneled sitting room with a small home office in one corner and a settee that can serve as a bed for the overnight guest. The random-width paneling is stained a medium-dark red, and lighter shades of red appear on curtains, blind, cushions, and rug. Touches of white appear on table surfaces and the bell-shaped glass lampshade. The settee is a striking design in cream-colored rattan, and this Malaysian touch is repeated in the cane and bamboo construction of the tables and chair. The scene outside may be wintry, but the mood inside is tropical.

areas of towns and villages, houses tend to be rambling, with sun porches, attics, and large basements that are just a memory to the modern city dweller. If you live in such a house, make the most of it.

A sun porch, for example, often makes an ideal guest room. It is away from the main traffic of the house, and usually can be closed off for complete privacy. In cold months it is likely to be chillier than the rest of the house, but lined draperies and an electric heater will make it usable.

The conversion of garage to separate guest house has already been mentioned, but the garage that is attached to the house can often be made into an extra room with much less trouble. Such a room will, of course, have many more uses than just the accommodation of guests. If it is used mainly as a studio, a library, or a family room, be sure you reserve a few drawers and closet space for visitors.

Attic rooms and basement rooms are obvious locations for the extra bed. The main problem in the atttic may be decorating and furnishing the place so that it does not look like the hide-out for a Charles Addams character. Light colors and small-scaled furniture will do a great deal to make the space seem larger.

The main problem with the basement room may be that this is the children's favorite hangout. The guest is in danger of finding himself surrounded by bewildering toys and—in the early morning—by small, curious faces. If there's a guest in the basement, banish the children to the attic; if there's a guest there, too, you are perhaps overdoing the hospitality.

Fabric pattern plays a major role in this golden guest-room suite. The yellow walls make a bright background for the charming floral patterns of the bedspreads, sheets, and pillowcases; and the towels in tall closet with louvered door are color-coordinated with the other textiles. Tall lamp provides good reading light for both beds, and the handsome headboards add a strong decorative design.

A splendid, cushion-strewn divan can be created from the double bed that has been replaced in the bedroom by a queen- or king-size bed. Use a splashy fabric, pick up its colors in the cushions, and set the lounge on 4 × 4-inch blocks.

Consider all angles in your attic, then use them so they become an asset, as in this study and guest room retreat. The A-shaped space is fitted neatly with shelves and a bunk bed with deep storage drawers beneath. Bottom shelf has two fluorescent lights under it. Chains from ceiling hold one end of desk top; other end is attached to wall.

A guest who happens to be musical would be happy to be placed in the music room. Guest quarters were built into an alcove which was constructed of plywood. Fabric was stapled to plywood, sprayed with white paint, and finished with a narrow molding. Bed is single mattress and springs.

The living room as guest room

The city dweller may be just as gregarious as his small-town cousin who has guests in attic, basement, sun porch, and garage, but he's in danger of seeming a hermit unless he can play host occasionally and put up a friend for the night — perhaps his country cousin who has come to town to escape all those guests at home. The city apartment demands extra ingenuity in planning for extra accommodation— the living room may well be the only possible place that can be used.

The sofa bed is, of course, the main solution here, but the problem is not solved as easily as that. Closet space, table space, and drawer space should all be generously provided, and the biggest problem — privacy — is easily solved by use of a decorative screen.

The possibility of overnight guests is something to be kept in mind when buying furniture

for, and planning its arrangement in, a small apartment. If such guests are frequent, your living room should be arranged so that one small part of it can be thought of as the guest area, always ready to be made up quickly for extra sleeping quarters. For many valuable suggestions about dual-purpose couches and other double-duty furniture, see *Dual-Purpose Furniture,* Vol. 7, p. 1250.

Check list for hosts

The thoughtful host will take special care with the small touches that can spell the difference between real welcome and hastily-thrown-to-

The top half of one wall sloping to the ceiling is the only clue that this guest room is in the attic. A chair rail of burnished wood is set decoratively all around the room, its rich color matched by the beautifully finished headboard. Deep blue of the wall-to-wall carpet also appears in pillows and in the two lamps. This handsomely furnished room would be a more than adequate reward for the climb to the attic.

For a dash of panache, a scalloped canopy—reminiscent of the days when tall poster beds were draped for warmth. Oak cabinet of Early American design provides ample storage space. A special luxury is the bed table, the base of which slides under the bed so that the occupant is provided with an adjustable surface for reading or—if he's lucky—for the ultimate luxury: breakfast in bed.

gether billeting. Make sure the mattress is in good shape, the pillows plump, the linen fresh. Provide a bedside table, with room for a reading light, books or magazines, and perhaps a carafe of cold water and a drinking glass.

In the bathroom keep a few new toothbrushes, fragrant soap, toothpaste, and any other pampering toiletries you care to assemble. The tiny "guest towel" is universally despised— guests are likely to avoid it in favor of any large towel at hand, feeling guilty but getting dry. Provide them with their own large towels, the thicker the better.

Even a minor item like coat hangers can make a difference. Wire hangers are the well-known symbol of a third-rate hotel and a careless host. Keep plenty of thick wooden hangers on hand, plus pants and skirt hangers.

Once you have gathered together the essentials, the art of hospitality will be learned with practice. If you truly delight in having guests, your pleasure will smooth over any minor inconveniences. Occasionally, a guest may outthink his host, and arrive with sleeping bag and all provisions. When that happens, be grateful for his self-sufficiency, and let him bed down.

A son or daughter off to college means an extra room for guests at home. This cheerful room displays some of the student's books and music equipment, but has plenty of space left free for visitors. A sleek high-rise sofa neatly disguises the fact that it can open to a double-size bed, and the desk lamp is conveniently placed for late-night reading. With the addition of a freestanding mirror, the desk itself would serve as a capacious dressing table.

HALLMARKS

To Identify Treasures, Look for Craft Symbols on Silver and China

Hallmarks are the marks stamped or printed on objects to attest to their authenticity, purity, or date of origin. They are found on pieces of silver and gold flatware, holloware, and on china, although in the latter case the imprint is usually called a trademark.

The term "hallmark" originated in 1300 in England when, under a statute of Edward I, gold objects had to be tested or assayed for the amount of gold in them. Pure gold, like pure silver, is too soft to make into an object that can be used, such as a spoon, but apparently some goldsmiths were adding too much alloy metal to the gold. The objects were then sold as having a higher gold content than they did, allowing the goldsmiths to profiteer. Consequently, the goldsmiths' guild, or trade union, was required to test gold utensils for their purity. The tests were duly carried out in guild halls around England and the objects were stamped with a mark indicating that they were up to standard. That mark became known as the "hall mark" and the practice was adopted for silver objects as well.

The hallmark actually consists of several marks on the backs of objects made in England. One tells what the gold or silver content is, another where the piece was tested, a third who made it, and a fourth in what year. Collectors can authenticate their antiques by referring to these marks.

In the United States, gold and silver are not tested by guilds, but anything stamped "Sterling" is required by law to be 925 out of 1,000 parts silver, and objects of gold are required to indicate their purity in carats—the sign 18K indicates the piece is 75 per cent pure gold, for example. In addition, many manufacturers stamp the piece with their names to vouch for its purity.

The use of identifying marks on china is an old custom, common to both ancient Greece and China. The marks were first used to identify the potter, later to identify the dealers, factory, potter, painter, and other workers involved in production. Sometimes the marks also referred to composition and mold number. Marking porcelain was first legalized in France in 1766. Unlike the hallmarks used on metal, the porcelain marking system was not regulated or compulsory, hence the marks are not always reliable indications of age or origin.

Each symbol of an English hallmark means something different. In the top row below, for example, the leopard's head means the piece was assayed at the London Goldsmiths' Hall; "P" is the date letter for 1492-93; and last is the symbol of the maker, Sir Edmund Shaw, Goldsmith to Richard III. In the middle row, the leopard's head is followed by the letter "O," which in this shield stands for 1729-30; the lion passant means the piece is sterling; and the maker's mark is that of Paul de Lamerie. At bottom are the leopard's head again (Birmingham, Sheffield, and Edinburgh have other symbols); the date letter for 1800-01; the lion passant; a duty-paid mark; and the sign of Paul Storr, silversmith.

Plan Them to Be Charming
And to Expand Your Living Space

Hallways used to be neglected. They were often dark, dreary passages that led from one room to another. In older buildings, before air conditioning or central heating, hallways provided the main rooms with extra insulation from the extremes of weather. They were not for loitering in or admiring. Now, however, with new styles of architecture, hallways are often both decorative and functional. You can display pictures and art objects there and even use them as overflow party space.

Besides being the place where one parks outdoor coats and overshoes, entrance halls are currently put to other practical uses. They may be equipped with a bureau or credenza where silver, large vases and other useful gear can be

A long corridor leading from a master bedroom suite to the main living areas of this house provides excellent acoustical buffering. The actual distance between sleeping and living area and the interposition of two large closets and a bathroom furnish an economical noise barrier.

A wall of glass doors transforms a long narrow hall into a gallery. A pierced screen on the opposite side of the hall admits natural light into an interior room. If it can be justified by reasons of light and access, the gallery, either as entry or as display area, offers a rewardingly luxurious use of space.

A wall-hung table is the special feature in this hallway. Such a table can be made of many different materials. This one is made of marble and rests on wrought iron wall brackets. The hanging light fixture provides just the right amount of soft light for anyone wishing to use the mirror. The small antique-framed picture and the antique coffee urn are an interesting contrast to the more modern styles of the mirror and the lights. The flowers add a welcome touch of outdoor freshness.

stored. Closed shelves could hold table linens. Bins might be used to store athletic equipment. In an extra closet, dining table leaves, a card table, and folding party chairs could be kept.

If you have a wide entrance hall, this is a fine place to keep your books. Bookshelves filled with books and objects of art can make any hall look warm and welcoming.

A hallway between the main part of the house and the bedrooms can be used efficiently, too. If it is large enough it might accommodate a chest for out-of-season clothing or for extra blankets and bed linen. Again, it might be the best place for a telephone table and chair.

The hallway is the main artery of this house It links the living room, dining room, and the two bedrooms. The floor is green slate and can be easily cleaned. The plant shelf is made of concrete and was a porch step before the house was remodeled. On the ceiling is an accent strip of textured paper framed by pine strips stained walnut. Pictures and knick-knacks are on display along the length of the hallway wall.

This hallway also has a wall-hung table. It is a simple, straight-lined wooden countertop. A turned wood base and delicately curved wall brackets support it. Favorite antique accessories are displayed on the table and the old sailing ships, each enclosed in its own glass case, are shown to good advantage. The stools provide guests with a perfect place for putting on or taking off boots. They can also be used for extra seats wherever needed.

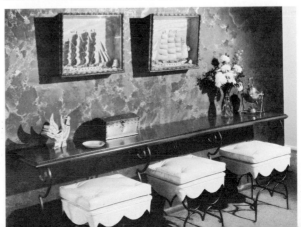

In contemporary architecture, open planning reduces the distinction between hallways and rooms. They flow more openly into one another and the hallway is often visible from the living room or dining area. Thus it may be the ideal place in which to feature a treasured antique—such as a highboy, a wall hanging, a grandfather's clock, or some other special possession.

Lighting is important in a hall. If you have pictures on the walls you might like to use a series of baby spot lights at ceiling level and train them on the pictures. If you have shelves, strip lighting under them is effective.

The hallway in this house is known as a flying-bridge hallway. It partially divides the entryway from the dining room and it gives an unusual accent to the whole middle section of the house. The skylight, which is directly above the stairs, provides natural light during daylight hours.

The 15-inch wall-hung table in this hallway solves a familiar decorating problem. The hallway is extremely narrow, thus most ordinary standing tables would be too wide and would block the flow of traffic. The table also provides a place for lamps that light this formerly dim area.

The pale, soft colors and interesting picture arrangement have transformed this hallway from the dark, gloomy passageway it used to be. The blue trim on the doors and the blue of the light fixture are a soft contrast to the cream color of the walls and floor. The plant adds a touch of fresh green.

HARDWARE

Choose Historic, Decorative Devices To Enhance Your Furnishings

Hardware is a word with a prosaic ring to it. It brings to mind utility, efficiency, forthright performance. And, indeed, the first duty of a knob, a hinge, a screw, a nail is to do its job properly. But after that, the design and decorative qualities of these humble servants enter the picture — and it can then be seen that hardware has a long and glamorous history and is a major tool with which to make plain chests, doors, and cabinets more attractive.

Hardware, like jewelry, is used to adorn and enhance. From left to right, below: an iron strap hinge, typical of Early American hardware; a drawer pull of classic design, a hallmark of Empire furniture; shaped brass backplate and bail handle, popular around 1720, especially associated with the Chippendale style.

The elegant sheen of brass or glitter of gold can add a subtle beauty to the items they adorn. Brass Georgian drawer pulls, bottom row, left, like so much Georgian hardware, were inspired by Chinese motifs. The spigot is a modern gold-plated bathroom fixture. Gold plating is a revival of a Louis XVI fashion.

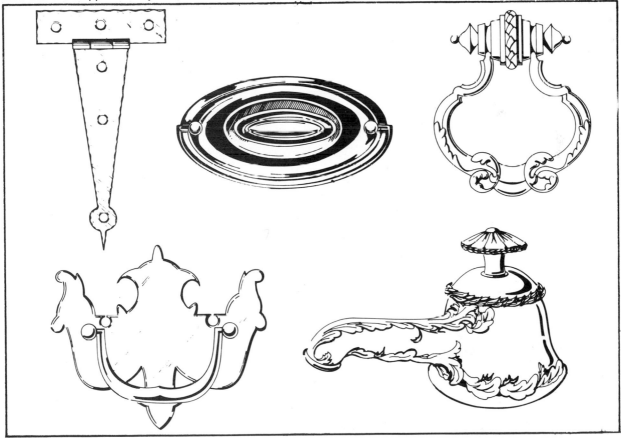

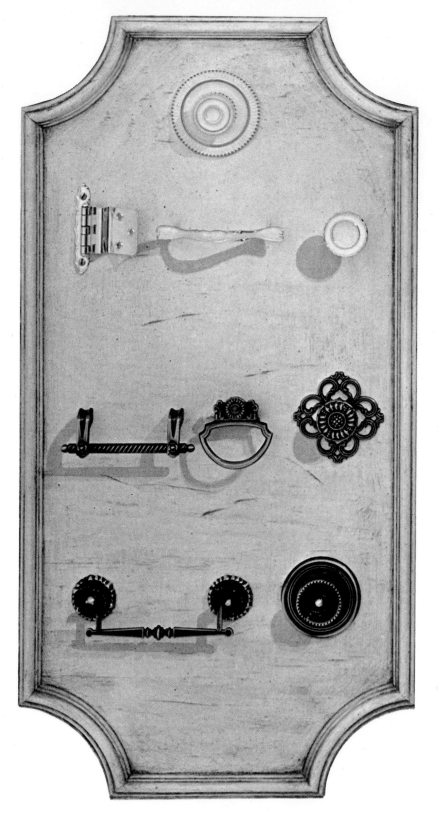

From the front doorknob and door knocker, right through the house, attractive, carefully chosen hardware can enhance whatever it is used on. Perhaps some of us are not as aware of drawer pulls, curtain hardware, hinges as we should be.

The Chinese were the first to realize that furniture needs hardware and that locks and hinges and knobs and handles can enhance the appearance of any piece of furniture. During the eighteenth century, in England especially, a great deal of hardware was copied from or inspired by the Chinese. During

The classic design of the knob in the top row illustrates simplicity and symmetry. The design is available in white or coppertone.

Queen Anne hinge, pull, and knob use motifs similar to those found on silver and china of same period. The pieces are sold in gold-rimmed white or black.

Spanish influence is quite evident in the intricately detailed hardware in the third row. These designs are available with or without the backplate.

Italian classic, less fanciful than the Spanish pieces above, has simple dignity. This hardware is available in gold, brass, or iron finishes.

Napoleon's day classic design inspired Directoire and Empire hardware, which was usually gilt-bronze. In addition to such obvious articles as drawer pulls and hinges, decorative hardware also includes drapery hardware: rods, rings, and tiebacks—available in a variety of styles, from Puritan plain to curvy rococo. Doorknobs, locks, and latches are also items of decorative hardware that can be used effectively indoors and out. Finally, bathroom fixtures: faucets, spigots, towel racks, clothes hooks, even soap dishes, constitute a large category of decora-

This French Provincial hardware lends an air of authenticity to any home. The hardware comes finished in antique copper, brass, or ivory and gold.

The Mediterranean design, center row, left side, again recalls the classic period. It usually comes in antique silver, brass, or copper, and satin black.

The openwork design of drawer pull and knob, center row, right, is ideal for a girl's room, dressing room, or bath. Suggested finishes: copper, brass, chrome.

Galleon silver and strong design point to Spanish origin in the finely styled hardware in the bottom row. These are well suited to a Mediterranean room.

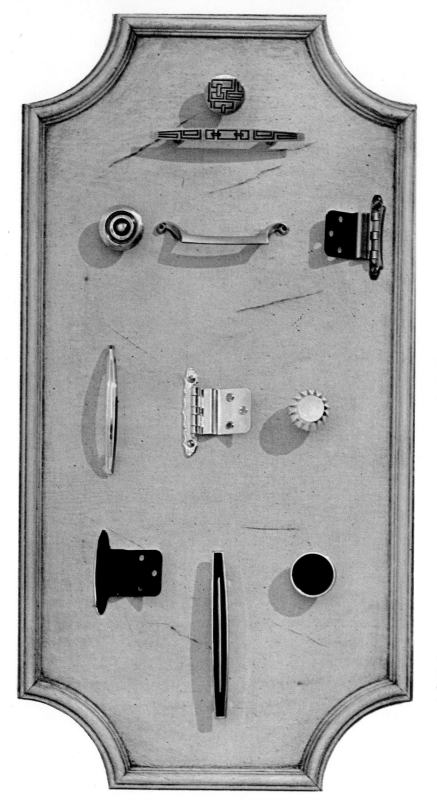

tive hardware. (Besides being available in metal finishes, bathroom fixtures can now be purchased in colored porcelain finishes, color-coordinated with bathroom tiles and linens.)

Today hardware is available in reproductions and interpretations of all the hardware styles that have flourished in the past. You may choose wrought iron or glass or bone, as a change from brass; or bronze; or gilt-bronze. Gold-plated hardware, stylish in the reign of Louis XVI, is back in demand, especially for bathroom fixtures.

Egyptian influence is strong in the engraved detail of the knob and drawer pull in the top row. The pieces are finished in silver, brass, and copper.

The flowing grace of the knob, pull, and hinge in modern style gives them a versatility that makes this hardware appropriate for almost anywhere.

White-and-gold drawer pull is a linear-leaf shape; hinge is designed in a series of brackets; and knob, available in white and gold, is in a lotus pattern.

The bold, stark line of the hardware in the bottom row is designed with an effective two-tone look. The centers are recessed for extra style.

The flowing lines of the larger brass drawer pulls are well suited to heavier pieces of furniture. The eighteenth-century reproductions on the double-pedestal desk above demonstrate the special combination of beauty and strength provided by metal hardware.

Curiously molded brass figure, reminiscent of Byzantine sculpture, is an unusual door pull. Where a more simply designed pull might be functional but decoratively insignificant, figure pulls such as this one add interest and life to an otherwise dull door or drawer.

Carved Swedish springerle boards, once used to mold traditional Christmas cookies, here serve as charming door handles for a modern kitchen cabinet.

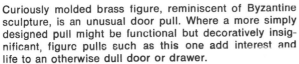

The bone-white drawer pulls add a distinctive contrast to the highly polished dark wood of the rolltop desk below. The small knobs are perfectly scaled to the dimensions of the desk and are in keeping with its delicate lines.

How to Find and Use Odd Ornaments To Dramatize Your Beds

Many beds are sold complete with headboards to match the rest of the bedroom furniture, but the day is past when the "matched set" or bedroom suite was the ne plus ultra of bedroom decoration. The options today are as wide as taste and imagination can make them. Headboards can be practical or fanciful; they can be costly and elegant; or sometimes, with the help of a creative eye and elbow grease, they can be *in*expensive and elegant. They can transform a small, undistinguished bedroom into a master bedchamber, or bring order into the sleeping quarters of youngsters. With a lamp attached, a headboard can provide a comfortable backrest that will invite the luxury of reading in bed.

Sources for headboards

Salvage and rescue operations are one source for unique headboard materials—and a particularly congenial one for decorators with a taste for reclaiming *lovely old things*. An auction sale or a thrift shop may offer an old, broken-down sofa—Victorian perhaps, or Empire—with the sofa back still in excellent condition, needing only to be detached from the broken frame and attached to the wall behind the bed to become a handsome headboard. The scalloped, carved, and gaily painted decorations from an old carousel can make the transition from fairgrounds to bedroom, adding a nostalgic reminder of an almost vanished age. Cellars, attics, country barns, and garages are good sites for treasure seekers to mine for headboard materials. Houses and old buildings due for the wrecker's ball are worth an investiga-

tion before their mantels, cornices, and paneling are irreparably smashed and cast aside in a junkyard.

The discerning eye can frequently uncover a scrap of fabric in a remnant sale, or a lovely curve of wood gracing a rocking chair now broken and abandoned in the attic. Almost everywhere, materials are at hand that can be recut, refinished, or rehung to reenter the world in a new guise—as a headboard.

Lovely old iron fences and decorative iron grillwork from balconies, so popular a century ago, now consigned to the junk heap, will reward the refinisher with a one-of-a-kind headboard at modest cost in effort. Invest in extra fabric and have a headboard upholstered to match the bedspread—particularly successful with spectacular fabric that is a standout among muted surroundings.

Comb the attic and basement for furniture discards that can provide decoratively turned armrests or legs to be wall-mounted above the bed. Invest in two large cushions (measure the bed first, and buy cushions large enough to span the width of the bed) and cover them to match or contrast with the bedspread, or with other fabrics used in the room. Make a trip to any drapery department for hardware and poles to mount the cushions on the wall above the bed.

An antique French lit clos, once used to frame the entry to an enclosed bed recessed in a wall, becomes a striking headboard. Green leaf-patterned fabric is used for open space in the center of the headboard, the tailored bolsters, and dust ruffle. Area rug is closely related in pattern and colors.

Part of an old iron fence becomes an intricately designed headboard (opposite) when it is brought indoors and restored with care. More time and effort than dollars are needed to effect the transformation. Straighten bent parts into original shape and cut off unneeded parts. Remove rust thoroughly before painting. Mount the wrought iron section to the existing bed frame. The black pattern of bold curves and spear-pierced circles stands out dramatically against the red wall.

One decorating point, well made, was the principle employed in furnishing the bedroom below. The headboard is upholstered in an elegant fabric combining crisp blues and greens, and the same fabric is used for the bedspread and the bolsters. To point up this impressive material, the rest of the room is muted in color. Pale green striped wallpaper and white furnishings are unobtrusive.

From something old, something new. Two sides of an old bentwood rocker, rescued from a resale shop, were used to make this headboard (below left). The frames were simply polished and fastened to wall. White walls and a subtly striped spread in purple, red, and lavender keep the mood lightly sophisticated, as do the bentwood chairs.

Foam pillows covered in velveteen and hung from a wooden closet pole make an inexpensive but effective headboard (below). Buy the end knobs and support brackets for the pole in any drapery department. Lamp hangs from ceiling hook.

Organize children's toys, books, treasures with a homemade storage headboard divided into cubbyholes to hold everything from badminton racquets to sailing ships.

Apply fabric or wallpaper remnants to inexpensive fiberboard screens and attach wall brackets with hanging lamps. The construction will be easy to take down and move to another location in the future.

If you prefer an all-new headboard made to specifications and designed to a certain function, the locale of your search might shift to lumberyards. Or at the lumberyard you might simply buy decorative molding to add to a board you already own.

A headboard can be large or small, the dominant focal point or a minor accessory. Choose it with care to accomplish the effect you desire.

Above all, a headboard is a practical convenience. If you have ever slept on a studio couch that had none, you will probably agree that it is much more comfortable to lean against a headboard than against a wall.

Measure accurately

Before a foraging or a shopping expedition, it is a wise precaution to measure and jot down the width of the bed for which a headboard is needed. Standard bed sizes are: twin (39x74 inches); long twin (39x80 inches); full (54x74 inches); queen (60x80 inches); king (78x80 inches).

King-size can be approximated with two long twin mattresses and springs, or two box springs with a foam- or spring-type mattress. A queen-size mattress and spring can be used with a standard double-bed headboard—a new one or your old one. The 60-inch queen-size bedding will project an inch or so on either side of this headboard. If you are also using a double-bed footboard, use bed stretcher rails to lengthen and widen the frame for the new queen-size box spring. If, on the other hand, there is no footboard, use a queen-size bed frame mounted on casters—this can be attached to the double-bed headboard.

Small bedrooms without strong architectural interest are the rule rather than the exception

Simple shelf system (left) for a couple of boys derives its rough-and-ready good looks from the massive 2 x 6-inch planks used in its construction. A piece of plywood covered with vinyl fabric fits between the uprights to make an effective headboard. A wood stain finish completes the design. Desk lamps placed above the headboards invite reading.

A budget headboard (below) for a rented home provides lighting that can be moved later. Two fiberboard screens (four panels each) have frames painted dark olive. Fabric glue was used to apply fabric to the panels in alternate solids and stripes. Wall brackets and tubing were screwed into framing to hold lamps. Easy and inexpensive to do yourself.

in many new homes and apartments. At the same time that bedrooms have grown smaller, beds—the ones most of us want—are larger. The two trends create a problem; how to fit queen-size or king-size beds into rooms that sometimes seem midget-size.

One solution that works well is to use an entire wall as a backdrop for the bed, making it the undisputed focal point of the room. Equip this wall with storage and lighting facilities that work together to provide most of the necessities and amenities for dressing, reading, and, of course, sleeping.

A large bed in a small room means there is little space for other furniture. Recently there have been a number of fresh ideas worked out in bedroom furniture design, resulting in cunningly crafted pieces that take up a minimum amount of space. Units that stand unobtrusively against the wall open up to reveal cabinets, closets, drawers, even a dressing table that folds out from a flat position, with its own plate-glass mirror sliding into place at the same time.

With cleverly designed furniture like this available, there is no need to be intimidated by the size of your bedroom. By using a minimum of furniture and accessories and concentrating on one focal point, you can lessen the feeling of confinement which an overcrowded small room can create. The headboard, a decorative item often overlooked when planning bedrooms, can be used to great advantage as the focal point. The pictures on these pages should give you an idea of how effective and decorative headboards can be.

A bed with a low headboard gains drama when it is placed against the windows, where a window shade that rolls up from the bottom serves as a backdrop. Shade adjusts by cord and pulley system, permitting privacy and light control. The narrow-striped fabric used for the bedspread and the window shade creates a unifying sweep of pattern. Elegant brass pierced lamps mounted over the bed provide excellent lighting for reading in bed.

The Householder's Guide to Warmth In the Most Efficient Systems

After mortgage payments and taxes, the heating bill is the largest annual household expense for most homeowners. Ironically, those with the highest bills may be getting the least for their money—because of an inefficient system. With modern heating, we should expect simply to set the thermostat and enjoy a constant level of comfort no matter how cold the temperature outside. If you are not enjoying such ease of comfort, maybe it is time to update your heating system.

This is one home improvement job where you have to rely mostly on the experts. The controls and equipment that make up a modern automatic heating system are quite complex, and they must be carefully selected and properly installed to meet the particular requirements of your house if they are to perform according to expectations. But don't call in the pros yet. First, let's explore some of the possibilities.

If your furnace is a relic—say vintage '55 or earlier—just about any unit you buy will be an improvement. Today's models are quieter, cleaner, and far more efficient than their ancestors. But a furnace that is only a little better than your present one may soon be obsolete. Homeowners are rapidly coming to consider such "luxuries" as central cooling, humidification, and air cleaning as necessary as central heating. When you are thinking about replacing your furnace take the opportunity to upgrade the climate all over your house.

Shopping for a system

Start shopping before your old furnace has had its last breath. Visit the showrooms of several heating contractors, compare the brands of equipment they handle, and evaluate their service facilities. Pick up manufacturer's brochures and study them carefully.

You should narrow the field to two or three contractors and invite each of them to your home to give you an estimate. Make it clear that you are interested in quality as well as price and that you want a top-notch *system—* that is the key word.

A "total comfort" system will include many extras. Do not panic at the list of equipment recited by the estimator—you need buy only the basics at first. By planning for the whole system, you can add on later at relatively low cost.

Ask for an itemized estimate so that you can decide what to do without or what to postpone until later. This allows you to tailor the installation to your budget while still getting the best possible heating system for your home.

Extras

What about those extras? In a forced-air system, for example, a central cooling unit can utilize the same delivery system, but cool air requires larger ducts than warm air. If your updating project involves the installation of new ductwork, make sure it is large enough for cooling purposes; the actual purchase of the cooling unit can be put off for a few years to stretch the dollar outlay.

Humidification and air cleaning are other important functions that a total system can perform. (See *Moisture Control,* Vol. 12.) An electronic air cleaner in the furnace's return plenum can remove up to 95 percent of the airborne dust in your home, drastically reducing your cleaning bills, not to mention day-to-day cleaning chores. This unit is particularly valuable if anyone in your family suffers from allergies. But it is an add-on and need not be part of the original installation.

When the estimator totals his estimate for your system, make sure he includes an installation guarantee, a yearly maintenance contract, and free call-back service for balancing and adjusting after the work has been done. When you are making your decision, be sure to keep in mind that you don't have to do the whole project at once. But hold onto that estimate—it's your blueprint for year-round comfort.

Gas versus oil

The controversy rages on: which fuel is better, gas or oil? The flames of argument are fanned by expensive advertising campaigns waged by the utilities and oil industries. Actually, both modern fuels, used in efficient modern burners, will provide clean, safe heat. All other factors being equal, natural gas would get the nod because it requires less complex equipment and less service. But all factors are rarely equal, and the controversy is largely a consideration of economics and the region in which you live. Costs of each fuel vary widely across the country. If you are faced with a choice, get estimates of annual costs from fuel suppliers and your heating contractor. Some gas companies offer a guaranteed estimate—no charge if your fuel consumption exceeds a predetermined amount.

If gas-burning equipment is used it should carry the seal of approval of the American Gas Association. This guarantees certain safety measures. Also, a safety device should be attached to the pilots of all gas-burning equipment. This ensures that the gas valve will be closed if the pilot light should go out, thus preventing the escape of gas.

Electric heat

Electric heat is both practical and popular. In many sections of the country, it is as cheap as heating with gas or oil, and it offers several advantages, particularly cleanliness and flexibility.

The individual room system is the most common type of electric heat installation. Units are built into each room, and each room has its own thermostat. Baseboard units are most popular, but heaters may also be built into the floor, wall, or ceiling. Another way to heat individual rooms electrically is to make the heater an integral part of the ceiling. Insulated heating wire is looped back and forth across the ceiling and covered with plasterboard. There are also prefabricated heating panels of plasterboard and a system in which a copper heating mesh is sandwiched between flexible vinyl sheets that are pasted to the ceiling like wallpaper. With a radiant ceiling, all heating equipment except the thermostat is concealed.

Central electric heating systems are also available—similar to the conventional hot-water and hot-air systems. And large, central heat pumps can heat, cool, ventilate, dehumidify, and even cook. Your local electric utilities company is the best source of information about the costs of heating your home electrically.

Heating the add-on-room

Add-on rooms have a heating problem because most of them have three exterior walls; so the weatherproofing and heating must be above average to keep the room comfortable. Insulation of walls and ceiling, use of double-pane glass or storm sash on all windows, and weatherstripping of doors and windows are essential.

Central heating, supplied by the home's furnace, is the best source of heat for the add-on room—if the furnace has the capacity to handle the job. Your heating contractor can advise you on this. If your present system can't take the additional load and if you are not ready for an all-new system, an individual room system is the answer. There are several types available. For most situations, an electric unit is the best choice for cold-weather comfort in the add-on room.

How to Fit Your Sound Equipment Into Your Decorating Scheme

Sound waves first were harnessed late in the nineteenth century by Thomas Edison, who invented the phonograph or "talking machine." The largest feature of early models, an oversized ear trumpet, soon became an instantly recognized symbol of the new scientific triumph. Since that day, the art of sound reproduction has been steadily improved and refined until today it represents an intricate mix of art and science, an electronic tool putting music at everyone's fingertips.

Music for everyone

Hi-fi and stereo are a new leisure resource, a means by which music previously difficult of access and performers who once had limited audiences have been made widely available. Fine music and musicians, once heard only by aristocrats at court performances, and folksongs once brought only to local towns by strolling troubadours, can now be heard almost anywhere and at almost anytime by anyone with the relatively modest price of a record.

Home libraries of music rivaling, even outdistancing, the finest music available to royal patrons of the past are not out of the ordinary today. The vast and ever-growing collection of recordings and tapes runs the gamut from the classic music of Bach, Beethoven, and Brahms to popular hits, poetry readings, and speeches of history-making importance. Worlds of music, the great literature of the past, Broadway musicals, ethnic music, and the top-forty favorites of teenagers are on records and tape.

The number of people with a taste for recorded entertainment has increased greatly as the quality of the equipment has improved and as prices have dropped to a level many can afford. Today millions of devotees buy the needed equipment and spend many hours enjoying it. Home record parties, evening musicals, dances—and the electronic equipment, record and tape libraries needed for these activities—are important new factors in home decorating.

Housing the components

The equipment must be housed with an eye to its appearance and an ear to its acoustical needs. Records and tapes must be stored, and a comfortable listening environment must be created. Happily, turntables, speakers, amplifiers, and tuners lend themselves to a number of satisfactory arrangements. They may be treated as separate components and placed on open shelves or concealed in cabinets. They may be concentrated in one room or scattered throughout a number of rooms.

A comfortable listening environment may mean high-backed easy chairs, or it may mean a bare floor for dancing and cushions for lounging while listening. If the equipment serves an owner who is not yet permanently settled, it may be conveniently stored in easy-to-move, portable units. If space is precious, the hi-fi equipment might be stored ingeniously, using a piece that does double duty as a coffee table. If the decor of a room is traditional, components may be built into an old armoire or antique chest. If music is an all-important part of a family's everyday life, the electronic equipment may be combined with a piano or organ

Here a freestanding wall unit adds exciting architectural dimensions to a once boxlike room and gives this family a much-needed music wall. The wall is made up of a tension pole unit system placed around an electric organ. Since the entrance door is at the left, a hall develops behind the units. The cabinets of the wall system provide storage, and shelves hold an amplifier and speakers for the stereo turntable resting on the lower cabinet. Furniture is arranged to face the music wall focal point. Shaggy brown carpeting covers the living room floor while the hall is floored with vinyl tile. Blue walls set off the buttoned, black-leather sofa and blue cushioned low-back cane chairs. The large glass-top coffee table seems to float airily. A Chinese horse on the shelf above the organ is a perfectly placed work of art.

Twentieth-century paintings and art objects in many styles, plus some rococo angels and an exotic Near Eastern table, have been mixed in this eclectic family room where hi-fi components are mounted and displayed like the works of art. The wall is divided into four big blocks of brown and beige, which form a background of neutral wall tones for pictures, a collage, and the hi-fi speakers. Tape deck and tuner-amplifier arrangement are mounted separately at desirable heights for good listening and easy use. Plump winged cupids are pure decoration, as are the pop art ketchup, mustard, and beer bottles on the speaker and coffee table. Bare floor is wood planking. A tray of beaten metal serves as a coffee table.

in a music wall that is the focal point of the living room. Whatever special needs are being considered when the switch is flipped and the music rings out, the hi-fi or stereo should bring increased pleasure to everyone in the home.

Hi-fi and stereo installations are wonderfully flexible and can be incorporated into traditional or wildly eclectic rooms, and into large or small spaces, creating a "listening environment" for dining, for conversation, or for concentration on the music. A conventional living room, too small to accommodate an extra piece of furniture, can have a hi-fi added without sacrifice of comfort or loss of charm in the room's decorating scheme. Simply use the unit to replace an existing piece of furniture and let it do double duty as a coffee table or a pair of end tables flanking a couch.

A family with a limited dining area and a taste for soothing dinner music might mount a speaker inconspicuously in the dining room, relegating the turntable, amplifier, and tuner to another space some distance away. In a large family room, the hi-fi components can be an integral decorating element, displayed like works of art. Components are wall-mounted or set on shelves, each placed for aesthetic interest and ease in handling. Solutions to the problem of installing a hi-fi depend on decor, on space, and on whether the music is to be actively listened to or to be played softly as a background to other activities.

Concealed by a cane and walnut screen, this speaker is located in the dining area, a considerable distance from the source of the music, which is the coffee table hi-fi in front of the couch. (See picture bottom left.) The separation prevents an overcrowded look and diffuses the sound throughout the living-dining room.

If saving space is important, you will be interested in this way of housing hi-fi in a coffee table (below, left). Caned sides and ends are used to reduce the bulky look that a solid wood piece would have. The hinged top holds cigarette box and a cornucopia spilling leaves, with plenty of space for records.

The hinged sections over the recessed control panel and turntable (below, right) can be flipped open easily from the sofa, leaving ample table surface for accessory pieces. There is no inconvenience with this fingertip music control.

On a short wall jog between floor-length windows of the living room and brick wall of the entry, a floor-to-ceiling installation to house a turntable, amplifier, speaker, and two shelves of records. The turntable fits into a pull-out drawer for convenience in handling records; other units are behind doors.

With the doors and drawer closed, the hi-fi components present a panelled face to the world. From top to bottom, four sections contain speaker, amplifier, turntable, and generous record-storage space. Home carpenter can handily craft the cane-fronted drawer, door, and ceiling-high frame.

Often a music and hi-fi buff chooses to invest his money in tuners, speakers, amplifiers, and turntables, with little cash left over for decorative or expensive cabinetry to house the components. For this dedicated hobbyist, the best choice for storing and mounting treasured equipment is frequently to do-it-himself.

The do-it-himselfer need make no compromises with commercially designed cabinets. His speakers can be as large as he chooses and can be placed to ensure optimum results. His tuner, amplifier, and turntable can be as close together or as widely separated as he deems convenient or expedient. One choice is to expose the equipment to view on open shelves.

Much modern equipment is finely machined and assembled and has an elegance of its own that is as decorative as it is functional. The enthusiast who is proud of, and takes pleasure in, the beauty of fine equipment will enjoy having it on display. An alternate solution to housing a hi-fi set is to enclose all of it, or part of it, in cabinetry.

A cabinet has the advantage of protecting delicate equipment from accidental damage and dust. It can also blend in design with a room scheme in which the hi-fi components are out of place. If there are small and curious children with exploring fingers in the house, or if the location is unusually laden with dirt and dust in the air, a cabinet is a wise choice. Consider stacking the components in a floor-to-ceiling plan, placing the turntable in a pull-out drawer at waist height for convenient record changing. Place the speaker at the top of the stack—just under the ceiling for good diffusion of sound—and store the tuner and amplifier between.

A focal point has been created in this once-featureless room ▶ by paneling one wall. Random-width, wood veneer strips are featherweight, fastened with special adhesive. The shelf system consists of metal shelf support strips, painted wooden shelves. For heavy objects, such as the stereo tape deck, secure the metal strips with hollow wall fasteners.

A television set, records, and hi-fi components are important additions to a living room, but not always attractive enough to be on display. Here a tall, antique armoire was artfully transformed into a home for this living room entertainment center. Plywood was used to divide half the interior into compartments for the tape machine, tuner, records; the other half holds a turntable. All the vertical surfaces were finished with plush red velvet, a classic garnish for mellow woods. The whole unit has a custom, built-in look and can move to a new location with ease.

There is a very personal signature in this room at right, with a ▶ strong individual use of color, accessories, and lighting. Music is a major theme here, with the hi-fi components contained in one unit in a wall niche flanking the fireplace. The hi-fi's strategic location ensures easy use and good sound. The overall color scheme is cool white and green, warmed by accents of blond wood and wicker. A unique art object in white porcelain is displayed on a white wall above the mantelless fireplace, the purity of the setting a foil for the sinuous twining of the tree branches.

Stack-up hi-fi and record cabinets are a favorite system for storing components and record collections. These were a do-it-yourself project, using one sheet of hardwood plywood. Three boxes 16 inches deep, 16 inches high, and 30 inches long were made with perforated hardboard used for the backs. Next, hardboard sliding doors and aluminum tracks were installed. Matching hardwood molding was nailed to the front edges of the boxes to cover the plywood edges. Simple 1 × 2 wood frames between the boxes separate them and give them a floating look.

Quality equipment and careful placement

A trained ear, one that has been educated to finely reproduced sound, finds it hard to accept, much less enjoy, anything less than near-perfect sound, and for this, good equipment is an essential. Fine electronic equipment can be a major investment and requires much research and planning on the part of the owner, who may be justly proud of the results he achieves. Almost as important as the equipment is its placement in the room. Good acoustics are necessary for true high fidelity, and components must be located with an ear to the resulting sound. It is important to have the turntable easily accessible for changing records. Finally, all parts of the system—turntable, tuner, amplifier, speakers, and records—must be attractively displayed.

Make a Decorating Virtue Of Your Hobbies and Collections

A famous doctor, Sir William Osler, once said, "No man is really happy or safe without a hobby." It may be more true today than it was when he said it in 1905. Hobbies, whether they involve making things or collecting them, growing things or engaging in sports, help keep us interested in life and act as safety valves for the tensions we all experience.

Because hobbies enable us to express our individuality and because we like to live in surroundings that reveal our personalities, one of the best ways to make sure our homes bear our own individual stamp is to decorate and plan rooms with hobbies in mind. If you like to paint, weave, make furniture, mat and frame pictures, or bind books—among innumerable possibilities—organize a whole room, or at least a corner of a room, where you can work and where you can store the tools of your hobby. The ideal work area is one where you can leave work in progress out in the open. It is tedious to have to put everything away after each working session. Besides, if your work is ready and waiting, you are more likely to snatch odd quarter hours to indulge your hobby—and these spare minutes can add up to quicker results. However, if the room where you work serves other purposes and must be kept tidy, at least provide adequate storage space that is easy to get at, and where everything you use fits comfortably.

If the results of your hobby are suitable for display, place some of them around the house, not just in the room where you work. Use walls, shelves, cabinets, bookcases to exhibit your handicraft or your collection. In short, hobbies can be a decorative asset in your home. Some hobbies even develop from an object that was obtained in the first place as a decorative accessory. Many aquarium and terrarium buffs date their interest in exotic fish and glassed-in gardens to the time when they bought one or the other as a pretty accessory for the home—and gradually found themselves enthusiasts with a hobby.

This room is a hobby center for the whole family. The large clerestory window provides northern light for the painter, whose current work rests on the easel; open bookshelves hold the bookworm's favorite volumes and display the sportsman's trophies; and a games table is placed in front of the sofa. Cabinets provide plenty of storage space for everyone.

Part of this family room has been planned for use as a sewing center where sewing materials, fabrics, and patterns can be left out in the open ready to use while a particular project is in progress. The cutting-sewing table was made from an old, weathered door that was surfaced with plastic and set on metal legs. The protective plastic covering ensures that the table surface will be flat and safe from mark-

ings by scissors and razors. Wicker storage shelves are particularly useful because they let you see at a glance where supplies are stored and make fabric and patterns readily accessible. An old standing mirror in the right corner is a useful aid in fitting garments, and the hooks on its frame make a convenient place to hang unfinished ones. Items from another hobby—poster collecting—hang on one wall.

Many wealthy collectors have gathered assortments of paintings, furniture, or other treasures, and some of these collections have become famous; but millions of other people who collect things as a hobby do so at relatively little expense. The objects they seek may even cost nothing, like seashells or stones smoothed and shaped by ocean or stream, or interesting minerals that are fun to hunt for, exciting to find.

It might be said that if it exists, someone collects it. Currently, great favorites are the old tools of such trades as sailmaking, horseshoeing, and boot making; glass paperweights; the diverse patterns of pressed glass; old dolls with china heads; old coin banks; and old toys.

Any of these things and a myriad others that you might collect can be used to enliven your home. A rule of thumb for displaying a

Toy soldiers are so small that they need to be kept in groupings for emphasis. In this temporary arrangement the lancers prance spiritedly across a living room lamp table. For permanent display, the fragile lead pieces, only ½-inch high, could be effectively arranged in a wall-mounted shadow box, or in any glass-fronted cabinet.

When a hobby becomes so engrossing that it takes up most of the hobbyist's spare time, it can develop into a full-time profession. When this happens, the time has come to convert a room for the worker so that it measures up to professional standards. This attic, transformed by an enlarged window, vinyl floor, and cabinets, rivals a commercial art studio.

collection of small items is to keep it together in one place for maximum impact. And if it is a collection of tiny or fragile articles, display it behind or under glass—in a cabinet, or collector's table with a glass top, or glass-enclosed shelves.

Perhaps one exception to what may be artistically displayed is barbed wire. It is estimated that over 100,000 Americans collect the barbed wire that was used to fence the West in homesteading days. There are about 400 different kinds of early western barbed wire and a book has been written about it for collectors.

A collection of old cooking utensils—muffin tins, graters, ▶ trivets, gelatin molds—forms an interesting pattern on the walls of this modern kitchen. When arranging as many pieces as this for display, the collector should be careful to put the heaviest pieces placed near the bottom.

A drawing board is almost essential for the artist or designer, but it is also wonderfully convenient for any hobby that involves sorting or arranging or writing. A large, adjustable surface like this makes working a pleasure.

Kites from Japan and Taiwan, in the form of bird, butterfly, beetle, and fish, are inexpensive but impressive acquisitions in a youngster's bedroom collection, and are arranged to form a charming wall display. A few selections from the collector's hoard are often all the decoration a room needs.

Plan Carefully, Shop Wisely
To Make Your Work Center a Pleasure

Since adults as well as youngsters may have plenty of homework, they will need a proper place in which to do it. Every household has its share of letter writing, record keeping, and accounting. Some people bring work home from the office, others work at home full time. A well-designed home office provides a convenient and efficient place in which to work undisturbed by the normal home distractions.

The type, size, and location of your home office will be dictated by your specific needs and individual taste, as well as by practical considerations of space, room design, and pocketbook. A simple but adequate office need not require a great deal of money, time, or ingenuity to construct. It can consist of just a single piece of familiar furniture, such as a secretary or desk, or of a combination of tabletop and shelves. These pieces, placed in living room, bedroom, family room, or even in the kitchen, can turn a secluded corner or alcove into an office.

Renovate old equipment

The few pieces necessary can be picked up at sales advertised by stores specializing in commercial office furniture, or can be bought even more cheaply at secondhand shops. Desks, filing cabinets, chairs, and typewriters can all be found at reasonable prices with little searching.

Once assembled, the various bargains may look nondescript; but a day or two of working with paint, stain, plastic laminates, or contact paper can transform the furniture into attractive additions to any room. Investigate the great variety of modern materials that can make the job a pleasure.

Organization

The foremost requirement for a home office is proper organization. Well-planned storage areas require plenty of drawer and shelf space to minimize clutter. This is especially important if the office is in a central, much-used part of the house. If you want the office area to be clearly defined for what it is, let a handsome desk or sleekly styled piece of business equipment do the job, not a stack of documents or an accumulation of other work materials.

Ideally, home office space should be planned by the user, but if the designer is doing the job for someone else he should carefully consider the user's personality, work habits, and special requirements. Work materials like blueprints, charts, maps, account books, and large files may need special storage space, and smaller items like rulers, brushes, pens, and stamps should all be kept neatly in special compartments. Electrical outlets should be within easy reach for lamps and special office machinery.

Wall space can be put to good use in a home office. Use it as efficiently as possible for cabinets and shelves, a bulletin board, a wall telephone, or for displaying charts and maps. Shelves can be bought handsomely finished or as unfinished units to be completed at home. Unfinished or homemade shelves painted in bright colors provide a decorative accent to enliven the work area.

Some home offices boast an elaborate wall system combining drawers, cabinets, and open shelves. These modular units are available in combinations of wood, steel, chrome, and glass, in a wide range of prices. Most of them have adjustable shelves. In smaller spaces and for those with smaller budgets, a homemade book-

The family library, above, also serves as a comfortable, full-sized home office. The room is fully equipped with storage space for books and files, and its red walls, blue rug, and maple furniture combine to produce a warmth and cheer that make it an inviting place to work.

This handsome corner, though not as spacious as the full-sized office above, is efficiently organized with shuttered storage cabinets, adequate shelf space, and roomy desk to provide a compact work area. The top of the cabinet forms a long surface to hold small office equipment—plus a radio-record player for music while you work.

shelf of 2x4 boards balanced on bricks can be practical, effective, and, when carefully constructed, quite attractive—a perfect temporary solution.

Other home-offices areas

If living room, family room, bedroom, or den are inappropriate for working at home, there are other places to put a home office. It may well occupy a previously neglected area of the home. A section of the basement or attic, a cor-

Modern multicolored cabinets, topped with an L-shaped white counter, are arranged around two walls. The counter is at the same height as the top of the traditional desk, giving the complete combination a built-in look. The pattern created by the colored sections of the cabinets is repeated in the rug's pattern of colored squares. A bulletin board makes maximum use of wall space; two pole lamps light the counter.

ner of the kitchen, a space under a stairway, or even the entrance or hallway of a home may provide suitable location for an office area. Remodeling can convert unused basement or attic space into an attractive, pleasant, and efficient office center with either built-in or freestanding desk and wall units. Good lighting and space-saving office furnishings can make a handy work area from a wasted corner, whether it is under a flight of stairs or at the end of a hallway. For salvaged locations like these, use corner cabinets, shelves which tuck into a right-angled space, and either clip-on tensor lights or spotlights set into the ceiling.

The hidden office

In multipurpose rooms, one-room apartments, or any small living area, a home office may be set up so that it is concealed, when not in use, behind closed cabinets. Specifically constructed office furniture converts at a flip of the wrist to hide papers, equipment, supplies, and clutter. Swivel shelves, sliding drawers, drop leaves, and adjustable stands can conceal equipment as large as a typewriter or a television set.

A convertible office increases the usefulness and decorative versatility of a room, and assures the privacy of personal papers and work materials in even the most frequently used spot. Even such a simple device as a tall screen can be used for adequate concealment.

Shelves, work counter, and compartments with sliding doors all project just 18 inches into the room, turning this narrow corner into a wood-paneled executive suite with all the comforts of home. Television set slides back out of sight, typewriter hides away in top of compartment at left.

The office above blends modern style with old for an original effect. The desk is a model of modern efficiency, the cushioned contour chair provides modern comfort. Area rug of vermilion shag is another contemporary note. Old-fashioned features are the office clock and the double lamp, both adding some warmth and charm from the gaslight era.

Den offices

A home office located in a bedroom or den can permit more personal expression in its organization and decoration than a living room office. Family photographs and other personal mementos can be displayed, bulletin boards can be placed on the walls, and the various work materials in constant use can be arranged more openly. A more casual arrangement of furniture is possible, with greater freedom in choice of style. The den or bedroom office is generally in a part of the house not usually visited by guests or used for entertaining. For maximum privacy, quiet, and freedom from interruptions, this is the ideal location for your home office.

The living room office

Often the living room provides the most convenient place for a homework area, with the office occupying one corner or sometimes a whole section of the room. This may be an "executive center" for running the household, where family accounts and records are stored and where letters are written, or it can be an everyday business office for professional use.

When the same room is used both as a professional office and as a living room, the furniture and the color scheme must both be chosen with the double duty of business and pleasure kept in mind. Neutral tones or earth colors are ideal, and the clean lines of modern furniture

This freestanding one-piece home office, with a desk in front and doors behind, combines work and storage space in a single convenient unit. Underneath the drop leaf are three drawers. The gleaming stainless steel frame prevents the unit from appearing too massive, and the richly patterned wood grain adds decorative interest.

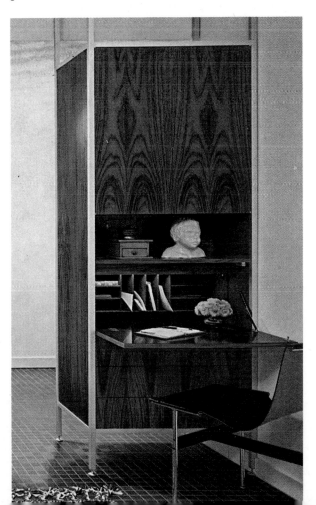

The three pictures down the left side of this page show home offices that consist basically of long slabs of working surface plus chairs and shelves. The corner at top is a fine example of modern styling, with a spacious worktop on stainless steel legs, overhead lighting supplemented by a slender desk lamp, and bookshelves against the wall behind the desk. Far end of desk has storage space underneath. The wall decorated with maps and print could also hold a bulletin board.

The middle picture shows a small bedroom office. A sturdy Parsons table provides ample work surface and leg room. The hanging cabinet, with tambour doors that pull across from the center, contains space for storage of reference books, bills, household records. Sleekly modern desk lamp and elegant armchair with upholstered seat complete the simple but well-organized arrangement.

Ingenious use of a slab door makes a do-it-yourself executive-size desktop in the bottom picture. One end is attached to the windowsill; the other end is supported by salvaged ornamental iron scrolls, their baroque curves adding unique contrast to the straight lines of the other pieces. Desk is placed so that it can be shared by two people, one on each side, with low-hanging ceiling lamp providing light for both.

Compact and comfortable, this room is an excellent example of the harmonious blend of convenience, function, and traditional styling. Wall unit is simple bracket and board combination, with shelves stained to match the period desk and ladder-back chair. Adequate lighting is provided by desk lamp and by floor lamp next to leather easy chair. Accessories such as fire bucket magazine holder and curved wicker seat add original touches of decorative interest.

Shelves made of 1 × 8 pine boards painted flat black and bracketed to the wall, a long table, and bentwood chairs painted bright yellow make a cheerful office. The mood is informal, but all equipment is at hand for serious work.

A more formal design is evident in this living room corner. The built-in wall grouping consists of a roomy desk, storage compartments, and shelves. Some of the wood surfaces were hammered and stained for rich, weathered look.

make this style a good choice for the dual role it must play. Natural materials such as wood, leather, and wool help to create a calm atmosphere, and ornaments should be few and unobtrusive.

If possible, one wall should be devoted to storage and work space. Desk, shelves, cabinets, and bookcases can all be placed against this wall; and if in its nonoffice hours the room is used as a music center, the electronic equipment can be placed here with the office equipment.

Lighting

Even the most attractive home office is a failure if the lighting is not efficient. Supplement the room's normal lighting with lamps for the work area. The type of lamp suitable will depend on the sort of work usually done in the home office

This corner has a pleasantly old-fashioned look, even though the desktop is made of Formica. Slat-back chair, tall desk lamp in style of old hurricane lamp, and wide-board side of desk itself all blend neatly with the high wainscoting and the floral wallpaper. Another reminder of bygone era is the pendulum wall clock with its large roman numerals.

They can be attached to the edge of the desk, to a nearby shelf, or to any handy ledge. Most of them are strictly functional designs of jointed arms, swivel heads, and knobs for tightening the lamp into position, but their no-nonsense construction often results in a better-looking lamp than one that attempts to be decorative.

A vibrant color scheme of cool turquoise and warm yellow in this living room creates a tranquil atmosphere conducive to work. The efficient storage unit at the left, holding typewriter and dictating machine, frees the desktop for paper work. The long overhead cabinet, reached by a sliding ladder, is both decorative and functional. Concealed lighting both above and below this cabinet gives it an intriguing floating appearance. The arrangement of sofa, chairs, and glass-topped coffee table makes this corner suitable for professional use.

The coordination of built-in wall shelves, cabinets, and desk ▶ units with an integrated lighting system of pole lamps results in an expertly organized home-office area. Wall units provide bookshelves and magazine racks as well as compartments for business files, while the glass-topped desk with its adjacent shelf extension offers plenty of surface space for telephone, typewriter, and adding machine. This arrangement is especially suitable when homework is heavy. Informal accents like the beer-stein pencil holder, the café curtains, and the tulips are a reminder that the office is also part of a home.

If you have only a few square feet to devote to an office, it's important to make the area a natural part of the room with the help of color and furniture arrangement. The handy office area below was created by using the desk to provide a low wall defining the office space; yet compatibility of design and color makes the desk and its chair an integral part of the room.

and on the space available. The Department of Agriculture recommends a minimum incandescent wattage of 150-200 for reading or writing and a minimum fluorescent wattage of 40-80.

If there is ample space, use a desk lamp for typing, writing, or study. The tensor type is excellent for work concentrated in one small area, though its high-intensity bulb is more expensive and has a shorter life than ordinary bulbs. For wider illumination, fluorescent tubes are ideal. These are best used in combinations of two or more, as the light they provide is not as steady as that from the incandescent bulb. It is a slightly flickering light; two or more fluorescent tubes offset each other, providing even illumination. The long, thin tubes lend themselves readily to concealment—under a shelf above the desk, for instance. For the pleasantest light, use fluorescent tubes in combination with incandescent bulbs.

Art supply stores sell a great variety of adjustable clamp-on lamps, and these are especially useful where there is no room for a desk lamp.

For a more elaborate arrangement, spotlights recessed in the ceiling are effective. They can be adjusted to focus on any particular area, but provide a more diffused light than the tensor lamps.

Avoid facing a window if you work in your home office during the day. The view may be pleasant, but window light direct in the eyes is almost a guarantee of eyestrain and headaches. Arrange your office so that the window light comes from one side or from behind.

The office area here is as impressive as the rest of the room. Its components: a handsome desk in the middle of the room, a bookcase, and cleverly concealed filing cabinets along one wall. The desk is placed against the back of the sofa, and the room is further divided by the suspended double panes of Plexiglas with two prints of equal size sandwiched between.

Spanish-Mexican influence is evident in this bedroom office. The dark, heavy desk, splendidly carved and with chair to match, is placed at a right angle to the wall, setting the work area apart from the rest of the room. Wood shelves on metal brackets are set against a large panel of black vinyl. Bright stripes of rug prevent room from seeming too somber.

With a Bit of Grit and Know-How You Can Make Your Own Heirlooms

Hooked rugs and their cousins, latchet-hook and needlepoint rugs, are enjoying a new wave of popularity in modern homes. They are beautiful and highly individual, and making them by hand is a satisfying and useful hobby. The finished products can be used as area rugs or as wall hangings; either way, they are like paintings in wool.

You can, of course, buy patterned rugs, and pretty ones at that. But you can get much greater variety in color and design, to say nothing of a sense of pride, if you make them yourself. It is not always less expensive to make your own rugs, even if you count only the money you spend on materials and do not include your time; but the cost of a rug you make yourself is only a fraction of the cost of similar handmade rugs offered for sale and has the added value of being the product of your choice.

None of the rugs is too difficult to make, and you can buy kits for all of them that include backing material with a pattern already printed on it, the right quantity of yarn, and instructions on how to hook the rug. Hobby shops and some department stores sell these kits. Those who are experienced at rug making often like to make their own patterns and choose their own colors to match background or accent colors in their rooms, and some shops will transfer a design that you have devised to the backing material for you.

Rug hooking is an ancient craft, but the patterns of present-day hooked rugs can have a contemporary appearance. The rug in the picture on the right, for instance, reveals a semiabstract flower pattern in four colors. Some of the colors are repeated subtly elsewhere in the room.

Automatic needles

Hooked rugs are made with continuous lengths of yarn drawn through a backing of burlap or soft monk's cloth with a hook very much like a crochet hook or with an automatic needle such as that shown on p. 1815. Instead of making each loop by hand and judging by eye to see that all the loops are the same height, as one must do with a simple hook, you let the automatic needle do it for you—at a much faster rate.

The automatic needle works something like an eggbeater. You guide the machine with your left hand, and with your right you crank a

An automatic needle makes uniform loops at a rate of up to 500 a minute. A frame holds the burlap backing taut, so you can use both hands to work—you guide the machine with your left and crank a handle with your right to activate the needles. Machines are available with up to ten settings for different heights of loops, but a medium length is best.

handle which activates a pair of needles. One needle plunges through the backing material to make a hole and the second needle carries the yarn through, making a loop on the right side (you work from the back) that will be high, medium, or low, depending on how you set the machine. This means that more than one person can work on the rug and there will not be a difference in the size or spacing of the loops. Consequently, this can be a real family project.

Automatic needles are adjustable, some of them for up to ten settings, allowing you to make different sizes of loops. Low loops are best for pillow covers, medium loops for rugs, and high loops for special effects. All three lengths can be used on one rug or wall hanging, and you can cut some loops after they are made, leaving others looped for more artistic effects.

Tracing the pattern

When you buy a kit that includes burlap backing with the pattern already traced on it, all that is necessary is to fill in the spaces with the right color yarn. The best way to do this is

The sinuous shapes in the rug above seem to grow like vines of mustard-colored yarn, blossoming in red and blue flowers with green leaves, all on a white background. The design is Early American—many excellent rug designs were created in colonial days—and it goes well in almost any setting.

Latchet-hook rugs

Latchet-hook rugs are made on a stiff, open-weave backing onto which short pieces of wool are knotted by means of a special tool—a latchet hook. Each piece of yarn is about 2½ inches long (you can buy it already cut) and is worked individually. You can use one color at a time to fill in the pattern before you do the background, or you can work in sections, changing colors as you come to the pattern, as when knitting.

The backing material has spaces of about ¼ inch. You can buy it plain and draw your own pattern on it with a thick soft-lead pencil— using the grid technique, designs may be transferred to the backing from illustrations of rugs or even paintings in magazines. You can also buy backing with the pattern printed on it. You work from the right side of the rug. This enables you to see the finished pattern grow under your hands, exactly as it will look when complete.

Hook your own Oriental-style rug on a burlap backing printed with Chinese motifs, as below. Like many authentic Orientals, this rug uses red, blue, green, and navy in a design that goes as well with period styles as it does with contemporary and even ultramodern rooms.

to outline all the shapes first with their appropriate colors and fill them in following the outline as you work. When the pattern is finished you can fill in the background color, working in straight lines until you come to the pattern, where you will have to meander around the outline. Irregularities of this sort will not show on the right side because the pile of the loops will obscure them.

When you have finished the rug, apply a latex backing—also included in the kit—to its underside. This makes the stitches permanent. Otherwise, you could pull one loop and unravel an entire section of the rug.

The hook is a hand-operated tool with a movable arm that works something like a valve: when you push the hook through a hole the arm opens and you catch a piece of yarn in the hook. When you start to pull it back through the hole the arm closes to meet the end of the hook and form a sort of noose that keeps the yarn secure while you hold the two ends of the yarn in your left hand. After you have drawn the yarn to the right side of the rug, push the hook through to catch the ends of the yarn and draw them toward you, knotting the wool neatly around a shank in the woven backing.

Mistakes can be corrected easily by removing one of the pieces of yarn and replacing it with the correct color. And you can tell by looking at the back of the rug whether you have missed any spaces, because you make knots on only the warp or the woof; if one cross-thread in the straight, even rows on the back is not covered by yarn, it is easy to spot.

Leave a hem of about 2 inches around the worked portion of the rug and turn it under when you are finished, mitering at the corners and trimming the seam to remove bulk. Then bind the hem with carpet tape sewn to the underside of the rug. No latex backing is needed because the knots are secure and will not come undone.

Needlepoint rugs

Needlepoint rugs are made on open-weave backing similar to that used for latchet-hook rugs but usually in a finer mesh, say ten squares to the inch, and a finer yarn, a three-ply wool referred to as Persian. They can, however, be made on a bigger or finer mesh backing, depending on the effect you want to achieve. Sometimes they can be made with a combination of different-sized stitches.

Backing material is available in three ways. It is sold plain by the yard, hand-painted with the yarn included in a kit, or commercially stamped with yarn sold separately. Some shops will paint onto the backing material a design of your choice, or you can do it yourself, using felt-tipped pens in various colors.

Needlepoint rugs are made with a tapestry needle—which is a heavy, large-eyed needle—and lengths of yarn which you cut to your own specifications (for ease in handling, 12 to 18 inches is suggested). Longer lengths will often twist and snarl. The stitch is called a tent or continental stitch.

The rugs are finished off in the same way as latchet-hook rugs, and some shops will do the job for you.

This bold, dramatic double-eagle pattern in patriotic red, white, and blue, in the rug below, is a strong accent for an entrance hall. The eagle motif is repeated on a pillow cover in different colors. Set your automatic needle for medium loops for the rug and low loops for the pillow cover.

Schedule the Jobs, Budget Your Time, Learn the Shortcuts

According to a survey made by an important Midwestern manufacturer of home care products, the majority of city homemakers spend 32 hours a week keeping house. In the suburbs this is reduced to 19.8 hours a week—mostly because there is less dirt than in the city. Results also show that cleaning the range and oven is the chore most hated by homemakers everywhere. In the city, ironing is the next most irksome job; in the suburbs, window washing rates second thumbs-down place.

Most women, however, are philosophical about housekeeping. If you want an attractive home, you certainly have to keep it clean and fresh. If you go to a lot of trouble (and most women do) to decorate your home attractively, you will not want the effect spoiled by dirty slipcovers, dusty lampshades, clutter on tables, or by soiled floors or stained rugs.

Good housekeeping saves money, too. Your furnishings will last longer if they are properly looked after. Know-how and good work habits plus a flexible weekly schedule keep housework from overwhelming you.

The basic tools

First, invest in the appliances and tools you need. Read all instructions thoroughly, then file them for future reference. Take good care of the tools of your trade—any skilled workman will tell you that care of tools is rule number one. Rule number two: store your appliances and tools in a convenient place and always return them to their proper niches.

To take care of your house efficiently you will have to know about different kinds of cleaning products: what to use for the laundry, what to use for windows and mirrors, what to use to remove stains from different kinds of fabrics.

Some tried and true products are still favorites: ammonia for glassware; paste wax and elbow grease for furniture—unless you want a dull finish, which is achieved with a cream polish; liquid wax-and-cleaner in one for wooden floors, which should be washed as seldom as possible. Wax is recommended for stone or brick floors, soap and water for ceramic tile floors. Many other kinds of flooring require specific cleaning products. Find out what you should use from your local dealer. Different paints also require different care. Consult your paint store.

A market basket makes a handy tote for all of the small pieces of equipment—jars, rags, brushes—you will need during a cleaning bout. Assemble everything and carry it with you from room to room. This saves steps and exasperation.

Professional procedure

Tips for wall cleaning: test both painted surfaces and wallpapers to find out if the wall is washable. Don't wash a wall starting from the top and working down; the cleaning solution may dribble through the lower dirty areas, leaving streaks that washing will not take out. Always wash from the bottom up.

Daily vacuuming is recommended for carpets and rugs where there is heavy traffic. It helps the carpet fibers to maintain tone. Do not let dirt collect more than one third down into the pile. When carpets or rugs are too dirty to restore by vacuuming, either clean them yourself with a product made specifically for the fiber in question or have them cleaned by a professional.

There is a professional way to clean mirrors and windows. Do not spray a light coat of cleaner all over the window, and do not spray in circles. Make an X pattern, with the spray touching the four corners of the frame. This pattern makes cleaning faster, gets into corners quickly with two easy motions, and saves on the amount of spray you need to use. A timer brought into the room you are cleaning will allow you to leave a dinner cooking.

A schedule that distributes the work load through the week is easier to stick to than a haphazard, clean-everything-in-one-day orgy that leaves you exhausted.

"Preventive" housekeeping

One way to make housekeeping easier is to decorate in a manner that lessens housework. Soil-shedding and stain-resistant fabrics and floor coverings, shrink-proof slipcovers, washable paints and wall coverings are all preventive products that cut down on scrubbing. Air conditioning helps to reduce dusting, and modern appliances and heating methods help to prevent build-up of grease on wall surfaces.

When you select furniture choose clean lines that have no crevices or grillwork openings to catch dust. Look for wipable veneers, leather-like washable upholstery (leather itself washes with soap and water), curtains that can be laundered and hung back on their rods without ironing, no-iron mats and tablecloths and bedspreads.

Use coasters to protect tabletops, wax wooden surfaces to protect finish, and cushion the bottoms of ashtrays, lamps, and vases with adhesive felt. Washable slipcovers will protect furniture during summer months, when family and guests are more casual.

Another method of preventive housekeeping is to put things away as they are used: hang up clothes after use and put soiled clothes in a hamper, for instance. If you have a place for everything, it *is* possible to keep everything in its place. This means your decorating plan should provide enough storage to avoid clutter. Use dividers, shelves, pegboards, storage units, closets, and cabinets with storage room.

If you have a collection of small objects on display, it will save hours of dusting and re-arranging if you display it behind glass in a cabinet, rather than out in the open. Keep magazines in one big basket or rack, rather than all over the house.

Organize the jobs

Organize the work by grouping jobs. If you are baking a casserole, bake a coffee cake for tomorrow's breakfast and another casserole to put in the freezer at the same time. Vary the day's jobs to avoid fatigue caused by monotony; and do not schedule two heavy jobs—e.g., ironing and window cleaning—for one day.

Dress for the job when you clean the house. Wear comfortable clothes that launder easily, shoes that are well broken in, rubber gloves to protect your hands.

Your schedule should cover daily jobs: air and dust and tidy up all rooms; make beds; mop floors and sweep carpets; clean the kitchen; check supplies; and if necessary, add to the shopping list. If you have a dishwasher, leave used dishes in it and run it once a day.

Once a week you should vacuum all rugs, change linens, wash or wax woodwork, scrub the bathroom, turn mattresses, clean the range and refrigerator, polish mirrors, wash the kitchen floor, brush draperies and upholstery, scour garbage cans, and launder.

You can see that setting up a schedule will help. An organized, professional approach to housekeeping will eliminate much of the drudgery and save a great deal of time.

With Proper Care and Feeding, Your Plants Will Prosper Indoors

Contemporary architecture is partly responsible for the growing popularity of house plants. The starkly geometric interiors of most office buildings and of many modern houses, with their wide expanses of glass, benefit a great deal from the color, softness, and graceful shapes of plants. Even banks, where formerly the only green was legal tender, are now lush with plants—and much the friendlier for it.

For people who have overlooked the decorative, sculptural qualities of plants, a whole new world is theirs to explore. Plants are yet another tool for the interior decorator to use creatively—and they seldom involve the same amount of investment as most other home furnishings or accessories. Their decorative usefulness extends from a single small plant on a table to a grouping that becomes the focal point of the room.

Cleverly placed plants can hide or at least minimize unfortunate room features like pipes or obtrusive beams; in summer they can camouflage an ugly radiator; and a mass of greenery can even serve as a temporary substitute for a piece of furniture you plan to buy, filling the space with its own kind of beauty.

Much beauty for little cost

As home accessories, plants can give a fresh look to any interior. This is particularly true in the summertime, when the greenery of the plants—and in some cases their colorful flowers—gives a room a gardenlike look and a feeling of coolness. Before embarking on this enjoyable decorating expedition, it may be necessary to shed some old theories. Some people avoid the use of plants because they think of them as expensive luxuries. They are, in fact, quite inexpensive when compared to many other accessories, and whereas a cheap bibelot is usually tasteless, even an inexpensive plant has beauty. The plant world has something for slim as well as fat purses, and your local florist or greenhouse proprietor is likely to offer friendly and helpful advice about buying advantageously.

Some people feel plants are too much trouble, but trouble is easily avoided by choosing those plants that require little care. Other people may be reluctant to become involved with plants because they hate to destroy even those that are obviously dying; but this sentiment is not shared by leading horticulturists, who recommend discarding a plant when it deteriorates. This professional attitude toward beauty as display—rather than as biology—must be developed by the person who wants to use plants effectively in the home. Even the outdoor gardener throws away annuals at the end of the season. In other words, it is necessary to accept the fact that no living thing lives forever. However, many house plants are a hardy lot that, with minimum care, will last for years. Some ferns have been known to thrive for twenty years and more in private houses and in public buildings.

This flamboyant plant is, like the pineapple, a bromeliad; the strong, spiky, shiny leaves are characteristic of the family. Yellow spot you see is the true, short-lived flower. Red bracts blaze on for up to three months. Plant needs medium amount of sun. Further details appear later in article.

Planters like this one give you an attractive arrangement of plants at two levels. The top row gets natural light from the window and the bottom row is taken care of by fluorescent tubes. Cabinets at bottom store fertilizers and tools.

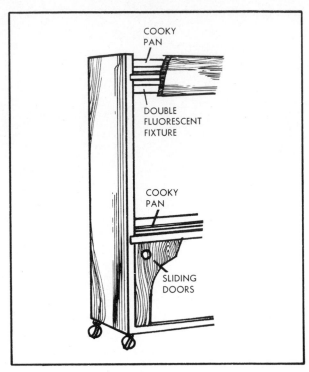

Diagram explains construction of plant stand. The cooky pans should be coated with rust-resistant paint, and lined with pebbles, which are kept moist. The plants are set on the pebbles and get needed humidity from evaporating water.

Indoor conditions

Plants can be grown everywhere in the house, and many will thrive as well in artificial light (fluorescent is best, but incandescent will do for some) as they do in daylight; but this depends upon the kind of plant. House plants are often simply lined up on a windowsill, an arrangement which is all right if they all need the same amount of light and can tolerate full sun. Many plants, however, have different needs, so you will have to be sure all plants in one group require the same light conditions.

Which plants you select should depend on where you live, how much time you want to devote to them, and what effect you want to create. In most American homes we maintain, for about half the year, an atmosphere of rather high heat and low humidity. The humidity can be increased in the plant area, of course, but the constant high temperature means that warm-country plants will do best indoors. Most northern, cool-climate plants need a winter of rest. Mountain laurel, hardy orchids, and trilliums, for example, simply will not live indoors through the cold season. To thrive in the house, a plant needs approximately the same moisture, light, and soil as it had in its natural habitat.

When a plant is first moved into the house, whether from your own backyard or from a greenhouse, or even when it is simply transferred from one spot in the house to another, it may react badly for a few days. This reaction will pass, however, and the plant will gradually accustom itself to its new surroundings, provided its minimum needs are satisfied.

A plant's needs are usually simple. Leafy plants need light, but little direct sun; flowering plants need sun in varying degrees; a few plants need special soil; and all, of course, need moisture (but you must take care not to over-water).

Literature and lore

For those who develop a plant hobby, there is a wealth of specialized literature on the subject. There are too many plant varieties to be fully described in this outline, but numerous booklets are distributed free or at nominal cost by botanical gardens, horticultural societies, and commercial nurseries. Societies have been formed that are devoted to almost every group of popular plants, and general garden clubs are popular everywhere.

For anyone who wants to explore it, there is considerable plant lore. For example, experiments have been made to measure the effect of sound on plants, with results that have convinced some people that plants can hear, and that music affects their growth.

Plants for every room

In the matter of plants as decorating accessories, there is something for everyone who can lift a watering can and for every room in the house. And nature's colors are easy to work with, from the many shades of green that most people find pleasing to the vivid colors of flowers that enliven a whole room.

Plants thrive in the bathroom because of the humidity, and they do a great deal to soften the customary glossy porcelain look. The theory that they should not be used in a bedroom is strictly an old wives' tale; it is true that during the night hours plants take small amounts of oxygen from the air, but the amount actually used by many plants in a room would be inconsequential.

Here is a happy solution for an empty corner or a bleak expanse of wall. The long wooden tray on top of the chest has been lined with aluminum foil to prevent leakage. It was then covered with a layer of pebbles or gravel to allow proper drainage. Water is occasionally added to this bottom layer to assure proper humidity. A fluorescent light fixture is suspended from ornamental iron brackets above. Plants shown include a gloxinia, a fern, and a snake plant.

Grouping plants on the floor along a wall base is an effective way to use them. Here, tall palms, medium-sized ferns, and low spider plants are placed in a well-balanced arrangement against a white wall, with wrought-iron sconces as part of the pattern. Necessary artificial light is partly provided by lamps concealed among the plants—the backlighting adds to the dramatic effect. The plain background is essential, of course, but the delicate floral pattern of the rug does not conflict.

The kitchen becomes a happier place to work in when it contains plants; and an entrance hall looks more welcoming when decorated with growing flowers or greenery. And, in the summer, plants that grow well in artificial light can make a pleasing arrangement in the fireplace.

Once the enthusiast becomes adept at plant-growing, the products of his skill will find their way into every nook and cranny of the house, either singly or in groups. When small plants are grouped together they help each other in maintaining humidity, while creating a more impressive effect than if placed separately. Large plants, however, especially the tall ones, can stand alone quite successfully.

There is a large variety of attractive containers for plants. Some simple household articles can be made to serve, such as ceramic bean pots, which make handsome cachepots; or glass bean pots can be converted to planters. You will probably need an electric drill to drill a hole in the bottom of any flower pot you invent.

Philodendrons (the smaller varieties), ferns, and grape ivy are among the leafy plants that grow well in hanging pots. Such flowering plants as begonias and geraniums, especially ivy geraniums, also thrive in this sort of container if you hang them in a sunny spot. Mixtures can be pleasing—a combination of different types of leafy plants can make use of various tones in a subtly effective way.

An ingenious plant composition has been made of this window area. One fairly large palm dominates the left side, and small flowering plants as well as glass and pottery are arranged on the right. The whole is framed in wood in a shadow box effect. The glass shelves are adjustable.

The asparagus fern is a good plant for cool rooms where the night temperature in winter does not exceed 55° Fahrenheit. Shady, moist conditions suit it, and soil should be compost of loam and leaf mold with a scattering of sand. Asparagus ferns are propagated by means of seeds.

Window locations

Windows are, of course, one of the most popular locations for plants, but even here discretion must be used, for most leafy plants do not like much sun (crotons and coleus are among the exceptions). Most flowering plants, on the other hand, like lots of it (begonias and African violets are among the exceptions).

The window arrangements can be simple or profuse—more elaborate groupings being possible at windows that are permanently closed. Although nowadays many homes do not have windowsills, it is quite simple to supply a substitute by building a shelf supported by brackets; or you can put shelves across any part of the window. For these higher shelves, glass is a good material. Another way to keep plants near a window is to hang them.

Consider, too, how much time you want to spend on the plants. Most (although not all) leafy plants do well if they are watered once a week and given some plant food from time to time; but a display that looks quite charming may be more trouble than it's worth if the plants have to be moved to allow watering and feeding. Actually, rules about how often to water are difficult to formulate: so much depends on the kind of plant, how well rooted it is, and environmental conditions.

Containers

Each potted plant should have some kind of saucer or dish under it to catch the water that runs through. If the pot is placed in another container, such as a tray, it should rest on a bed of gravel or pebbles so that the roots are not standing in water.

Containers for hanging plants should usually be light in weight. Baskets, which come in a great variety, are ideal.

A roasting pan becomes a planter after a scrubbing and painting. With its potted plants sitting on an inch of gravel for drainage, the pan is suspended from wire chains to act as a partial room divider between kitchen and dining area.

Two specimens of the popular bromeliad family. Because they are adaptable to almost any conditions, bromeliads are widely used as house plants. The leaves hold water in their cuplike bases, helping the plants to flourish in sunshine or shade. The bromeliad at left is an aechmea, at right a vriesia.

Once in bloom, a bromeliad can be left in the center of the dining room table, like the one below. Even in that reduced light it will thrive for weeks. For renewed vigor, give it a few days of good light now and then. The distinctively patterned leaves make the plant decorative even when it is not in bloom.

Since heat rises, the higher these hanging plants are placed in a room the more heat they will get—a factor of some importance in the care they will require. And there are other points to remember: Can they be watered easily? Can they get sufficient light? Can they be fastened securely?

While clay pots admit air to the soil better than plastic pots, the latter are a good choice for hanging plants. They are lighter in weight and they retain moisture, so the plants need not be watered as frequently. A good way to water these hard-to-reach plants is with a watering can that has a long, curved spout. You will soon learn how much water to put into the pot without having it run over. Of course, if your plants are hanging in places like a porch or a breezeway there will be no worry about dripping.

Care of plants

Taking care of plants is somewhat akin to cooking—with practice and experience, one acquires knowledge beyond any rules or directions, no matter how sound the rules are. There is good reason for this, because the conditions under which a plant lives vary and the adjustability of an individual plant to its surroundings also varies, just as the cake one bakes is affected by the vagaries of the oven. One who cares for plants learns, therefore, by trial and error when a plant needs water, food, and more or less light.

When a plant is first brought into the house, from greenhouse or from garden, or even when it is simply moved from one part of the house to another, there is usually a period of adjustment it must go through. Change of temperature, new light conditions, lack of humidity can all affect it, and its leaves may fall or turn yellow; but this is usually a passing phase.

Humidity

House plants—and also the occupants of the house—will benefit from raising the humidity to a higher level than is customary in most homes during the cold months. Methods of accomplishing this range from a simple pan of water placed on a radiator or heat vent to electric devices designed for the purpose. A few simple methods are listed below:

■ Arrange plants in groups. The cumulative moisture they give off will help them all.

■ Wash or spray the leaves with water, in the sink or right in the planter. If a cloth or sponge is used, support each leaf with one hand while washing with the other.

■ Allow fresh air to enter from outdoors. This brings in moisture and is especially helpful during the months the house is heated. Do not, however, let strong drafts of cold air blow directly on the plants.

■ Place plants on a layer of pebbles or gravel that is kept just covered with water. Make sure the level of water is not so high that the plant's roots are in constantly saturated soil.

Light and water

Light is essential. Most foliage plants do not require full sun, but most flowering plants, such as geraniums that are to be kept permanently, do, at least for part of the day; some holiday-type plants that are temporary inhabitants of the home, such as poinsettias, primulas, Easter lilies, hyacinths, and calceolarias, last longer if they are kept out of direct

The renewed interest in house plants has brought plant holders back into fashion. Holders are available in a great variety of styles and sizes, and many of them can be easily constructed. These wooden trays, 4 inches deep, have plywood bottoms and liners of galvanized metal.

This lazy Susan plant stand holds a display of African violets. The unit makes it easy to see that all plants get uniform amounts of light. Simply turn the entire shelf section halfway around each time you water the plants. Shelves are made of ¾ -inch plywood surfaced with laminated plastic.

sun. Artificial light, incandescent or fluorescent, may be used as a substitute for, or as an addition to, natural light.

Also to be considered is the difference in sun and light intensities in different climates. For example, the winter sun of a northern city may be regarded as medium or filtered light for a leafy plant, while the sun of a southern climate would be too strong for the same plant.

Water is also essential, but not too much. There are, unfortunately, no precise rules to offer for watering plants, but a reliable general rule is that most house plants should not be watered until soil 1/2-inch below the surface is dry to the touch. Overwatering causes more casualties among house plants than any other single factor and can result in rotting of the roots and final collapse of the leaves. The degree of wetness needed depends upon the kind of plant. The soil of cacti and other succulents must be kept much drier than that of African violets, ferns, and begonias, for example.

Neoregalias, above, are bromeliads with especially beautiful foliage. Stripes of green, pink, and cream more than make up for the smallness of the flower—a lavender bloom down in the base. To enjoy the flowers, place the plants on a low stand or coffee table for viewing from above. Latin name of these specimens is *Neoregalia carolinae*—but "tricolor" will do.

◄ Two bromeliads are on display here: the one in the background is the flaming sword—one of the few bromeliads with a common name. Lengthy flowering periods are characteristic of many of this group; the "sword," for example, is colorful for about two months. While waiting for it to push its way through the water in the base, use the base as a natural vase for other flowers—as in foreground example, where it is a receptacle for yellow daisies. The base will hold enough water to keep the plant happy for long periods. Bromeliads, in fact, dislike pampering, and once the base has been filled with water the plant can be safely left for two or even three weeks.

All eight plants displayed here are bromeliads. The selection gives a partial idea of the endless variations found in the *Bromeliaceae* family—both in flower and in foliage. All of them, however, show the characteristic spiky leaves. Bromeliads, natives of the tropical forests of Central and South America, often appear in such unexpected colorings and forms that they have the look of man-made art—their beautiful leaf designs and brilliant flower spikes seem to be sculptured. Leaf scale is almost the only house plant disease that attacks them. The cure: sponge foliage with warm, soapy water, rinse with clear water.

Experienced gardeners can often determine whether the plant is wet or dry by rapping on the pot. If the sound is dull, no water is needed; if the sound is sharp and clear, the soil is dry.

Basic watering rules

Water should be at room temperature or even a bit warmer, not colder. Some experts suggest that if the water in your area is heavily chlorinated you should draw it from the tap and let it stand for a couple of hours before using it on the house plants. The chlorine evaporates after the water is exposed to the air for a while.

Watering from the top is most convenient for most house plants or plantings. Wet thoroughly until water runs out of the bottom of the pot, to assure getting water to the roots. *Do not let the plant stand in water.* It may rest on moist gravel or pebbles as long as the roots

do not stand in water. If the plant is too heavy to lift out of its container or saucer and there is too much water at its base, a meat baster can be used to draw off the excess.

Another—and excellent—method for watering is to set the plant in water to about half the depth of the pot and leave it there until the soil at the top shows moisture. Then let the pot drain until no more water runs out and put it back in its container or saucer. Plants native to areas with high humidity can be watered with a gentle spray—the shower is most convenient for this.

The following points concerning plant watering are worth remembering:

■ Plants that are native to hot, sandy places— cacti, for instance—need less water than those that originate in moist climates, such as palms and ferns.

■ Plants need less water when resting—that is, not blooming or growing.

◀ An indoor courtyard makes a pleasant breakfast area. A room like this could be constructed in most houses and even in many apartments. The flagstone floor is bordered by a serpentine curve of brick inside of which is a layer of white pobbles. If a plant area like this is installed in a room where leakage would be a problem, a metal liner should be installed on the floor before the pebbles are spread. The array of plants shown here is provided with good drainage by the pebbled strip, and the balanced design of high and low plants creates an interesting pattern. Large panes of translucent plastic conceal fluorescent lights that help nourish the plants while giving an effect of screened daylight.

The paper-white narcissus, harbinger of spring, can be started in winter in a dark place. Its delicate star-shaped flowers and simple culture have made it the favorite spring-flowering bulb for forcing. Middle picture shows African violets on a lazy Susan, arranged with pots of devil's ivy. The rare combination of beautiful foliage and truly outstanding blossoms distinguishes the African violet as one of the aristocrats of house plants. The violets need good light with full sun in winter but require shade from the stronger sun from spring to fall. At right, teacups form tiny jardinieres for newly started caladium tubers. The bright, intricately veined foliage of variety Rosalie is put to decorative use on a dining room table.

■ Plants in sandy soil will need more water than those in heavy soil with humus in it.

■ Plants in red clay flowerpots, which are porous and allow moisture to escape (and create humidity), thus preventing root rot, need more frequent watering than those in porcelain or plastic pots, which hold in moisture.

■ Plants need more water in hot weather or in a hot room than in cool temperatures, and plants in the sun need more watering than those in the shade. Sun-loving plants are usually the flowering variety.

Plant foods

Food or fertilizer should be used with discretion, and directions on the package should be followed explicitly. In other words, do not overfeed. Good commercial fertilizers come in tablet or powder form soluble in water, or in liquid form. Instructions, in addition to specifying quantities, often recommend how frequently to feed the plant. The experts are not always in agreement here; so, besides following instructions, you should observe carefully how your plants react. When liquid fertilizer is applied, soil should be wet.

Many soil elements contribute to plant growth, but the three that are found in most fertilizers are nitrogen, phosphorous, and potash; their proportions are listed on the labels in that order—*e.g.*, 10-6-4. Nitrogen aids the growth of shoots and leaves, and is essential for green coloring; phosphorous promotes flowers, fruits, and root development; and potash strengths the stems and often helps prevent diseases.

Another way to give a plant nourishment is to give it some new soil from time to time—twice a year is usually sufficient. Remove about 2 inches of soil from the top of the pot and replace it with new potting soil, which can be purchased ready-mixed—the most convenient renewal method. Be sure to leave space at the top of the pot (about half an inch) for watering.

Repotting

Some house plants thrive if they are potbound; that is, set with roots tightly crammed

Lily-of-the-valley is a favorite temporary house plant, another of the lovely specimens that can be started in the house to make spring seem nearer than it is. The tiny bell-shaped flowers have a strong fragrance, and the polished green leaves twist gracefully to a delicate point. Long after the fragile white flowers have vanished, their distinctive scent seems to linger. The pips can be ordered by mail complete with instructions and sometimes with moss for planting.

Double the beauty of your plants with an unusual plant ▶ platform of wood topped with mirror. Casters underneath make the device easy to move around. There are only four plants in this display but the reflections enhance their decorative effect and add an illusion of height. Any plant arrangement would benefit from this mirror construction; the specimens here are a small pickaback, a schefflera, which has relaxed "hands" of grouped leaflets, and two spathiphyllums, which occasionally produce lilylike flowers.

into a comparatively small pot. When roots begin to push through the bottom, that is the time to transplant to a larger pot, which also gives the opportunity to add new soil at the bottom.

To repot, invert the plant, and, holding the base of the plant between the spread fingers of the hand, tap the rim of the container on a table. If it is stubborn and refuses to leave the pot, push at the plant through the drainage opening at the bottom of the pot with a pencil or similar tool; thus loosened, the plant will come out almost intact.

Into the new pot (which should be absolutely clean and preferably sterilized with boiling water) put some pieces of broken flowerpot or a layer of gravel for drainage. Cover this drainage material with a layer of dead tree leaves, straw, or moss to prevent the soil from clogging the drainage; then add new soil. Place the plant on top, disturbing the roots as little as possible.

Since the pot is larger than the old one, you will need to add new soil around the plant. You can also discard some of the soil from the top and add new, taking care to leave adequate space at the top for watering.

In the case of very large, treelike house plants, you need a place like a garage or some outdoor area, and possibly the help of a strong man, to do the repotting; or, your local nursery may do this for you at quite reasonable cost.

Destroying insects

Gardeners like to say that every plant has its bug, but house plants of good quality are relatively free from destructive insects, especially if the foliage is kept clean by spraying or washing. You may come across these two pests from time to time:

■ Mealy bugs—these look like tiny white cotton balls and are probably the most common of the house plant pests. They can be destroyed by dabbing them with rubbing alcohol. Use a

The tall plants behind the sofa are kentia palms—hardy and well-suited to home growing conditions. Placed on a high table, as here, their height is emphasized, and their slender fronds form a lacy canopy over the seating area.

small swab of cotton rolled around a toothpick. Do not use much alcohol, and confine it to the bugs, getting as little as possible on the leaves. For the first treatment, try diluting the alcohol with equal parts of water. If that does not work, use undiluted alcohol. While the bugs are on the plant, isolate it from the other plants.

■ Aphids—tiny insects that sometimes appear in clusters on the underside of leaves or on stems or buds. They may be red, green, black, or gray. These and other insects are best treated with an insect spray bomb available at most florists and nurseries. If the infested plant is not very expensive, the best thing to do is get rid of it and replace it with a healthy one.

Other helpful procedures

■ Plastic covers: plants can be left for several days—some even for several weeks—while the owner is away if they have been watered well and covered with plastic. The small plants can be covered with ordinary plastic bags used in the kitchen; larger ones may need sheets of plastic fastened at the top. Put a few stakes in the pot to keep the plastic from resting on the leaves.

■ Remove foil: some florists like to wrap plants in foil in an attempt to glamorize them, but the foil keeps out air and should be removed.

■ Propagation: cuttings that are used to create new plants should be from fairly new growth, and should be taken from the sides of the plants. Some cuttings grow roots in water, some in sand, others in heavy soil. These baby plants should always be kept out of the sun.

■ Bringing indoors: plants that have summered outdoors should remain there until just before the first frost. Before bringing them inside the house, spray them thoroughly to get rid of bugs. This is also a good time to trim plants. If they need tying up, use sticks camouflaged with green paint.

■ Setting outdoors: when plants that have been inside are placed outside the house, set them on a piece of tile or slate to prevent worms from entering the drainage hole.

■ Disease: the only disease—as distinct from infestation by insects—which occurs often enough to consider here is caused by soil-borne, rot-producing organisms. As there is no effective remedy, a plant that has this disease should be destroyed promptly.

■ Growing seeds indoors: because insufficient humidity is the greatest hazard in successful germination of seed grown indoors, a glass lid or plastic cover over the pot is helpful. As seeds germinate, gradually slide cover off and let air circulate.

This former breezeway was converted into a lushly planted dining area. The plant wall, facing streetside, is mostly window. The angled panes admit plenty of light for the plants, and the mottled glass preserves privacy. Plant area would also be good place to grow herbs.

For looks and fragrance the hyacinth (a caladium is in foreground) is one of the choicest bulbs to force. There are hyacinth bulbs on the market which flower indoors if grown in water, but there is greater danger of bulb rot with this method than if bulbs are sunk in soil outdoors and brought indoors to flower. Remove plant from full sun before flower heads open.

Popular house plants

Thousands of different plants are popular for indoor use (one directory lists 7,000), but comparatively few are available everywhere or suitable for all areas. Following is a short list of hardy house plants that may be found in most parts of the country; your local plant expert can undoubtedly suggest others. Since house plants are usually chosen for decorative purposes, some indication of size of the foliage plants, as well as suggestions for attractive groupings, is given.

FOLIAGE HOUSE PLANTS

12 to 36 inches high

An asterisk (*) indicates the plant is also available in sizes 6 feet or more.

Aglaonema (Chinese evergreen)
Bromeliads (many varieties)
Cacti (and other succulents)
Caladium
Cissus (grape ivy and kangaroo vine)
Citrus* (orange, lemon)
Dieffenbachia (dumb cane)
Dracaena
Ferns (asparagus, Boston, holly)
Ficus
   Elastica* (rubber plant)
   Lyrata* (fiddle-leaf fig)
   Nitidia*
Monstera
Palms
   Kentia*
Peperomia
Philodendron*
Pittosporum*
Podocarpus*
Pothos (devil's ivy)
Sansevieria (snake plant)
Schefflera*
Spathiphyllum (has white flowers at times)
Spider plant (hanging plant)
Tolmiea (pickaback)

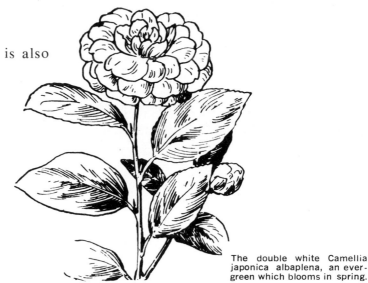

The double white Camellia japonica albaplena, an evergreen which blooms in spring.

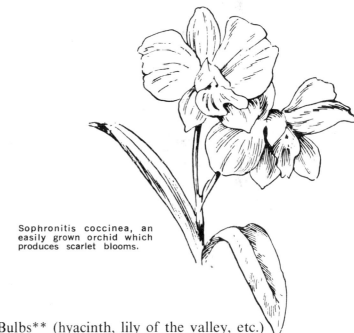

Sophronitis coccinea, an easily grown orchid which produces scarlet blooms.

FLOWERING HOUSE PLANTS

Double asterisk (**) indicates plant can produce blooms in the house. They all need sun part of the day. Most of them thrive in temperatures of 55 to 60°F., and almost all have foliage attractive enough to make them effective as decoration even without bloom.

African violet**
Anthurium**
Begonia**
Bromeliads**
Bulbs** (hyacinth, lily of the valley, etc.)
Camellia
Cyclamen**
Gardenia
Geranium**
Gloxinia**
Orchid**
Poinsettia

Beauty from the desert

All cactus plants are succulents, though the reverse is not true. Succulence in a plant means the ability to store water, and it is this ability, along with its heat-reflecting shiny coat, that permits the cactus to thrive in the desert. The slightly waxy outer skin covers leaves and stem; small cells inside the skin are a barrier to the escape of water from larger cells that store food and water; and scattered throughout the mass of inner cells are tubes for conducting water up from the roots, and other tubes that carry food in both directions.

Cacti may be a special taste, but when in bloom they can be as vividly beautiful as many of the more popular house plants. The well-known Christmas cactus, for instance, is a welcome plant to have in the house in mid-winter, for it blooms then into a display of flowers that are large and deep red. Its leaflike stems tend to hang, so it should be placed where they have room. It is a good plant for a hanging basket and will benefit from a summer spent outdoors.

All cacti and other succulents like to be warm and dry. They like the sun and just enough moisture to keep the top of the pot wet. They do not do well in the ground except in sandy soil where water drains off quickly; similarly, the pots they are set in should allow good drainage.

In addition to those shown here, there are thousands of other succulents, some of the more popular being the peanut cactus, orchid cactus, crown of thorns, jade plant, and the aloe. All of them are excellent house plants that require a minimum of care.

Cacti can be fed the same plant food as other plants—except when they are resting, rather than flowering. Most of them rest during the winter—the Christmas cactus being an exception. They are subject to mealy bugs and scale insects, but less so indoors than out.

Although they originate in the desert, cacti should be potted in standard potting soil mixed with sand (but not seaside sand, which is too salty). If sand is not available, mix the potting soil with crushed brick or finely broken flowerpots to assist drainage.

Some cacti propagate better from seeds, others propagate better from cuttings. Spring and summer are best for taking cuttings, since plants are then in a growing phase.

Many of the plants grow offsets at soil level. For these, you need only detach the offset from the mother plant and insert it in soil that is half coarse sand, half garden loam. Keep it dry a few days, then water as usual.

Succulents, which include cacti, come in a great variety. At ▶ left foreground and at right on the wall are echeverias displaying their rosette shapes and the flowering stems they produce during the summer. The other two plants on the wall are examples of the small, beadlike sedums.

Single plants in the succulent family may be unimpressive, but in a grouping they can create striking effects. Echeverias, sedums, agaves, and aloes are some of the heat-loving succulents shown here. Be sure to bring succulents indoors well in advance of winter weather—one light frost kills them.

The caladium is one of the impressive house plants with leaves of many colors. It needs filtered sun and will grow to about 1½ feet. Soil should be kept moist but not wet.

Ivy geraniums will often do very well in a sunny window. Here they are paired with a daisy plant. They are also extremely effective in a hanging basket or pot.

Gift plants

Plants have always been popular as gifts for special days such as Easter, Mother's Day, and Christmas and as a cheerful note for the sickroom. Florist shops are full of flowering varieties that make welcome gifts. They are lovely and, though their lives may be limited, everyone enjoys them.

There is, however, another dimension to plants as gifts that is worth exploring: consider giving the longer-lasting foliage house plants, or plants for a garden, or special plants for the hobbyist. These often answer a difficult gift problem in a new and satisfactory way.

Almost any newly married couple would welcome a good-quality plant of the medium to tall size, since their new home is apt to be lacking in furniture and accessories. Look over the list of recommended house plants on the preceding pages and then consult a reputable nurseryman or florist.

If your weekend hostess has a garden, it is hard to go wrong by taking her a plant—a rose bush, hydrangea, azalea, or other hardy type that has been forced into early bloom by the florist. After it has served its purpose as an indoor decoration, it may be planted outdoors in the garden. If there is no garden, select a permanent house plant.

Many women are baffled when it comes to buying a present for a man, but men like plants—and they're a safer choice than a tie. As mentioned at the beginning of this article, modern architecture is greatly enhanced by decoration with plants; the man who spends much of his day in an office should be pleased with the gift of a plant to soften his surroundings.

Geraniums range in color from commoner reds to white, pink, ▶ and lavender. The potted plants do best when allowed to become quite dry between waterings, which should be thorough. They will often thrive in a sunny window and are perfect for window boxes.

Terrariums

Setting up a garden enclosed in glass is an adventure in artistic gardening that requires a deft hand and a good eye for arranging plants to the best advantage. You can, of course, buy a terrarium or have one made for you by your florist. As a gift, they are sure to please, whether you make them or buy them.

Putting the plants in place requires planning, so it is a good idea to have the arrangement laid out in the order you want before you begin to set the plants. It is best to place small plants in front and then build up to the taller one. The following plants are adaptable to glass-covered terrariums provided the devices are ventilated sufficiently to prevent moisture accumulating on the inside surfaces of the glass: African violet, maranta, begonia, coleus, croton, dracaena, ivy, peperomia, small philodendron, and palm.

Some people have success with woodland plants such as dogtooth violets, Dutchman's breeches, seedlings of evergreens, and varieties of mosses and mushrooms, but these are not suitable for very warm rooms; they do best where the temperature at night is 45° to 55° F. and by day is a few degrees higher.

Be sure to space the plants so they will have room to grow. Try not to get soil on them; if you do, use a soft brush to clean them off when the arrangement is finished. The soil must then be watered. It will need watering again only at rare intervals—about every few months. The glass cover should be lifted if excessive moisture gathers on the sides of the container.

Terrariums need sun, but in limited quantities—that is, bright light but not direct sunlight. Turn the terrarium from time to time so the plants get equal light.

A brandy snifter can be ideal for a small terrarium. You can also use fish tanks, bell-shaped domes like those in great grandmother's parlor, or any other clear glass receptacle that will show off the plants to advantage and will also permit a cover to be used part of the time. Dry, hot air of the house in wintertime is no handicap to plants in the terrarium, where moist air is trapped. Begin with a layer of charcoal, add 1 inch of gravel, line sides with moss (green side out), and add mixture of garden soil, sand, and peat moss to a depth of 1 ½ to 2 inches arranged to make a slope along the sides. If the top of the container is narrow, use tweezers to arrange plants. Place the glass garden in good light but not in full sunlight—this would trap too much heat. Since moisture is so well conserved, a glass garden needs little water.

Leave cover open for air
Taller plants at rear
Small plants at front
1" of gravel

Use glass cover
Soil
Line sides with moss
Charcoal

Plants for specific areas

To make the most effective decorative use of plants, choose them to fit a specific part of the house. Before shopping, have some sort of decorating plan in mind; knowing what type of plant you want for a certain room will help prevent impulse buying.

The average modern house is built with ceilings lower than those of older houses. Today's ceilings are generally about 8 feet high, and the furniture in the room is usually scaled to this height. A tall plant, however, will not be amiss in such a room; rather, it will create an illusion of height, and the form and color of its foliage will supply an unobtrusive pattern.

A plant that is 5 to 6 feet high is effective when standing free; used this way, it can be as impressive—and as space-filling—as a tall piece of furniture. The large rubber plant mentioned in the caption on the next page would be suitable for this purpose. Those of good quality are fairly expensive but will live for years if given proper care, so the cost per year becomes relatively small.

Bathroom humidity is beneficial to plants. In a large, lavish bathroom a tall plant will add to the opulence; in a smaller one, try a few pots of baby tears on a separate shelf or mixed in with colorful jars of cosmetics.

Medium-sized plants like the pickaback and the begonia are useful for filling horizontal areas rather than vertical. Peperomia, grape ivy, caladiums, and many others should be considered for this purpose.

Plants can be placed in many parts of the living room, just as long as they do not interfere with traffic and do not use up all table surfaces. Leave room for other accessories—especially ashtrays, because, contrary to a widespread notion, tobacco ash is not beneficial to plants.

In the bedroom, a small portable stand is a convenient place for plants—the sort of stand that can be carried with its plants to the sink when the foliage needs washing. With a layer of insulation as protection (asbestos shingles will do), you can grow many warmth-loving plants on a radiator top. Sansevieria, jade plant, and necklace plant, which tolerate rather dry air, would do.

Pickaback is a wonderful plant to have in the house because it seems to grow almost while you look. The name comes from its way of producing new plants at the base of old leaves, so that they appear to be riding on the back of the mother plant. It grows out more than up, and is therefore an excellent plant where you want width rather than height. It needs rich, well-drained soil with peat moss and leaf mold. The pickaback (*Tolmiea menziesii*) is one of the few popular house plants native to North America.

It is a pleasant occupation to work out the best arrangement of plants for different areas, and it is a creative element in any decorating scheme. Plants can be functional, too, when grown in a room divider where they are part of a substitute wall that separates space. Large plants can even form a divider by themselves, eliminating the need for construction. Another effective way to use plants is to arrange them with paintings—a real challenge to the artistic eye of the decorator. Sometimes paintings or prints in such an arrangement will look better unframed, with the plants themselves forming an intricate border.

The rubber plant is a tropical Asian tree (*Ficus elastica*) with strongly buttressed trunk that may exceed 100 feet in height. It is frequently dwarfed in pots for use as an ornamental, but the example here is dramatically high and adds a splendid mass of green to a room of high-voltage colors. The rubber plant is easy to grow. Hot, dry, or conditioned air does not discourage it; its chief dislike is overwatering.

Two hobby plants

Two plants that seem to lure people to become hobbyists are African violets and orchids, both of which are available in many varieties.

■ The African violet—The African violet does originate in Africa, but is not really a violet. The name derives from its color and the resemblance to our own North American woods violets. It comes in color varieties of purple, pink, and white; and its botanical name is *Saintpaulia ionantha*—in honor of Baron Walter von Saint Paul, who introduced African violets to Europe in 1893.

African violets adapt well to indoor life and bloom almost all the time. The best soil mixture for this plant is one-third each of garden loam, coarse sand, and of humus, leaf mold, or peat moss. An east or west window is usually best for light; direct rays of south sun may burn the leaves, and a north window, except in the summer, probably does not supply adequate light.

The African violet prefers a temperature of 70° to 72°; growth is slowed when house temperature drops below 60°. The plant can tolerate rather dry air but prefers high humidity—and for this reason is a good choice for terrariums.

Water the plant when the topsoil feels dry or use a wick-type container. The water should be at room temperature; cold water will cause the leaves to spot. A ceramic pot is ideal for the African violet; unglazed clay pots soak up harmful salts, and if this type is used the rim should be covered with foil to protect leaves.

The plants like an occasional shower bath—a fine spray of lukewarm water. Dust their

The ivies are surely among the most graceful of vining plants. They are attractive grown in a pot with a trellis or a piece of twisted wood to climb on, or—as here—in a low bowl where the tendrils can trail downward. Ivy grows either in water or in soil, and likes bright light. If the plant's regular location is poorly lighted, move the ivy into the sun occasionally. Keep soil slightly moist and temperature within 50° to 70° range.

foliage frequently, stroking gently from leaf base to tip with a pipe cleaner or a discarded leaf. Mealy bugs can be eliminated by touching them with alcohol as previously described. Propagation can be accomplished by inserting a severed leaf with a 1- to 2-inch stem into a pot of moistened vermiculite or coarse sand, or by inserting the stem through a cover of foil or wax paper into a jar of water.

■ Orchids—Contrary to popular opinion, the orchid—synonymous with luxury—does not require elaborate care. Two varieties that are recommended for beginning hobbyists are the cattleya and the epidendrum. Both are tropical American varieties; the former has flowers that are among the showiest known.

These plants do not need direct sun and will grow in artificial light. Buy the orchid from a reliable nursery and get specific directions for its care. It is an exciting event when the plant produces a bloom, which it does once a year. The nurseryman can give you a good idea of when particular plants for sale will bloom, and you can choose accordingly. Blooms last for weeks if kept in good light, out of the sun. Only if you supply greenhouse conditions of warmth and humidity will the plants bloom again. A good idea is to buy several varieties that will flower at different times.

In number of species the orchid family probably exceeds that of any other family of flowering plants. Orchids are found growing wild throughout the world, even as far north as Greenland. Species range from the humble lady's slipper to intricately fringed and spotted hybrids.

Because of the charm of the African violet, many new varieties have been developed in the last couple of decades. Blue Warrior, above, is an example of the newer types, and is particularly attractive because its blooms grow in a showy cluster centered above the leaves like a carefully arranged nosegay. The foliage of African violets differs from one variety to another, some more glossy, some more hairy than others.

Cattleya, the most popular orchid for corsages, is notable for its spectacular hooded flower, and is the recommended variety for beginners in orchid culture. It is native to the high altitudes of Central and South America, where temperatures range from 50 degrees at night to 75 degrees during the day and where humidity is quite high. If the hobbyist can control the environment, he should keep the night temperature between 55° and 60°.

Ferns

The fern class of plants has many varieties, all of them flowerless, but most of them attractive enough for home decoration. The luxuriant Boston fern is probably the best-known; other varieties are bird's nest, false hare's foot, holly, Victoria bracken, silver lace, and maidenhair—which is very beautiful but not a hardy type. Some of the smaller varieties are excellent for planting in terrariums, since ferns like a lot of humidity.

Ferns need daily watering of the soil plus a fine spray of water as often as possible to provide the necessary humidity. They should not, however, sit in water.

The plants do best if they are repotted once a year in fresh soil, at which time the roots can be separated and new plants started. They can also be propagated by cutting the side runners and putting these in about 1/2 inch of loose soil that is rich in organic matter—50 percent or more of peat is good, or equal parts of humus, loam, and sand with perhaps a bit of leaf mold and charcoal.

In general, ferns need filtered, never direct, sunlight. As natives of tropical regions, they dislike cold and thrive best at a minimum temperature of 65 degrees. They can summer outdoors in a shady spot, but be sure to spray for pests before bringing them into the house.

To make a table decoration for all seasons, top, combine two leafy plants of different forms. Here, the spear-like sansevieria planted centrally in a low brass dish is nicely contrasted with the heart-shaped leaves of a philodendron. In general, it is most effective to keep the taller plants close together in a clump, tapering the arrangement to the edges of the container with smaller, low-growing varieties; or, as here, use a vine like the philodendron to mingle with the taller plants.

The dwarf bonanza peach needs a planter that can sit indoors in full sun or outdoors—where it can even spend the winter in climates where little frost is experienced. This plant produces pink blossoms in the spring followed by heavy foliage of glossy, clustered leaves, then bright, full-size peaches at midsummer. This peach tree is an example of bonsai—trees or shrubs grown from a few inches to 2 feet or more in height according to classic forms established by the Japanese.

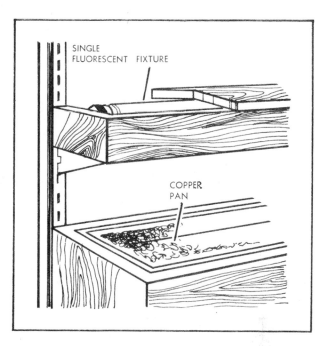

SINGLE FLUORESCENT FIXTURE

COPPER PAN

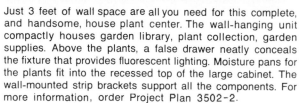
Just 3 feet of wall space are all you need for this complete, and handsome, house plant center. The wall-hanging unit compactly houses garden library, plant collection, garden supplies. Above the plants, a false drawer neatly conceals the fixture that provides fluorescent lighting. Moisture pans for the plants fit into the recessed top of the large cabinet. The wall-mounted strip brackets support all the components. For more information, order Project Plan 3502-2.

Of the many kinds of ferns used as decorative house plants, perhaps the one with the longest history of popularity is the Boston fern, once a standard fixture in conservatories and parlors. The fronds grow to a length of 2 feet and are from 3 to 6 inches broad. The plant adapts well to hanging baskets.

Plant containers

The ornamental stand known as the jardiniere was once the only acceptable container for display of plants. Today there is a far greater choice of receptacles—from the ordinary clay pot, undisguised and pleasing in its plainness, to a silver champagne cooler. Selecting, devising, or constructing a container is an added pleasure for the plant collector. All it needs is an open mind and a little imagination. A few ideas are listed here:

Muffin stands—these small three-tiered tables for holding food are ideal for small plants.

Toy wagon—once a child outgrows this plaything it makes a fine mobile planter.

Stoneware jars—formerly in wide use for preserving foods, these sometimes turn up at auctions. Their earth tones are a suitable foil for plant colors.

Bean pots—this heavy crockery is both sturdy and good looking.

Cookie tins—painted and filled with white marble chips, they make decorative containers for a group of plants on windowsill or floor.

Pots—copper or porcelain are especially attractive.

A dark-brown wastebasket makes an attractive container for the tall palm, which is in a saucer filled with pebbles. The small platform has casters for easy moving.

This double arrangement is two white stoneware containers set on one base. Spidery palms grow in one container; the other holds a low grape ivy plant.

Ficus plant at upper left has been set in a tall container to emphasize the plant's impressive height. In the foyer shown at upper right, the plants are imaginatively set at varying levels on slender metal rods. Below, a sturdy planter made of redwood holds a lush graptopetalum—a plant whose soft gray color accounts for its common name of "ghost plant."

Dishes—tureens, casseroles, chafing dishes, and other bowls.

Small trunks—can be painted and converted into excellent planters.

Baskets—all kinds, including bassinets.

Driftwood—partly hollowed out, a prize piece makes a beautiful setting for a small plant.

Plant boxes for both indoor and outdoor use are inexpensive to build and require no expert carpentry. Casters are almost a must if the box is primarily for indoor use. It is often advantageous to be able to move plants easily—from the place where they show off best to the place where they can get needed sun between showings.

INSULATION

Correctly Used, It Will
Keep You Warmer, Cooler, Richer

Insulation is one of the things that increases the value of a house. It helps keep your house warm in the winter—some estimates say it can save up to 40 percent on heating bills—and cool in the summer, whether there is air conditioning or not. If you are wondering whether to insulate your house, or the attic when you convert it for living space, you can be sure that the increased comfort and the fuel savings will more than offset the cost of installing the insulation; and the extra protection will add to the value of your house.

The purpose of insulation is to prevent the convection of heat. In the winter it will keep the heat inside the house, and in the summer it works in reverse, preventing much of·the sun's heat from entering. Properly installed, insulation will also check drafts, thus keeping floors warm and preventing dust streaks on walls and ceiling—all of which help cut down on housecleaning chores.

The physics of insulation
Although there are many different types of insulation, most of them work on the same principle: the use of dead-air cells. Air is the most effective preventer of heat convection known to man; if the earth had no atmosphere, for example, the sun would scorch our planet and nothing would be able to grow. Any material that creates pockets of nonmoving air insulates well. That is why mohair blankets are so warm—they trap air between their many wool fibers. As a rule, the smaller the cells of air trapped by a material, the more effective that material will be.

There are two basic classifications of home insulating material—cellular and fibrous. Cellular insulators are made of plastics or of certain minerals; fibrous insulators can be of either glass, wood, or mineral fiber. Different types of insulators are used for different applications, and a single house may use three or four different kinds of material. There is also, of course, a wide price range among the types, as well as differences in ease of installation.

The cellular materials
Cellular materials are considered by some contractors to be better insulators and a better value than fibrous. They consist of such plastics as polystyrene and polyurethane, and such minerals as perlite, which is volcanic rock, and vermiculite.

The plastics come in closed-cell, open-cell, or combination closed-and-open-cell construction. When the material is formed, tiny bubbles are created throughout, and when each bubble is a completely enclosed sphere, the material is called closed-cell. When a honeycomb effect is produced, it is open-cell.

Both polystyrene and polyurethane come in rigid forms to be placed between studs; and they are also available in liquid form to be sprayed into the stud space—a method of application called "foam-in-place." This is an expensive method, calling for the services of a contractor with a special machine, and it is used only for difficult applications.

Of the two plastics, polyurethane is considered better because it has more insulating capacity—perhaps twice as much—and therefore can be used in thin sheets, but it is generally more expensive. Neither polystyrene nor polyurethane attracts vermin and neither one rots; nor do they settle in place, which makes them good for vertical applications.

Although polystyrene and polyurethane do not burn, both melt at high temperature—polyurethane at 220°F., polystyrene at 170°F. Polystyrene is not recommended for roof applications. Polystyrene is effective against cold—more so than polyurethane—and is recommended for basement installations and under concrete floors.

Minerals such as perlite and vermiculite are available either in rigid sheets of porous rock or spun into loose fill of mineral wool. In either form they are noncombustible, but in boards they are sturdier, more stable, and will not move or shift once in place. Fill is good only for horizontal applications, such as underneath the attic floor. It is not good for walls—it eventually settles to the bottom.

The fibrous materials

Varieties of fibrous insulators include fiber glass, wood or cellulose fiber, and mineral fibers. The glass comes in blankets that are easy for the homeowner to install because the fiber is sandwiched between two layers of treated paper or aluminum and sold in rolls.

Wood fiber, which sometimes comes in combination with chopped-up cork, is the least expensive insulator but it has disadvantages: it is combustible, liable to rot, and may attract vermin.

Mineral fiber is rock that has been spun into a wool-like substance. It is moisture resistant, nonrotting, and undigestible by insects. It comes in bags, ready to be poured into place in a house under construction, or it can be machine-blown into the walls of an older, completely built house. Its main drawback is its tendency to settle.

Prices vary

The prices of the different types of insulating material vary from time to time depending on market conditions, but generally cellulose (wood) is cheapest; next higher in price are minerals, then polystyrene, and finally polyurethane.

An alternative to these materials is aluminum foil, which works by reflecting back into a room or to the outdoors the heat that is trying to pass through it. The foil is sold in inexpensive rolls. Attach it to studs with a staple gun, using one layer in warm climates, two or three in colder ones. It is also sold in combination with gypsum board: the foil is laminated to the back of the board so that insulation and wallboard can be installed in one step.

The vapor barrier

In rooms where a great deal of moisture is generated, such as laundries and bathrooms, it is a good idea to install a vapor barrier on the warm side of the insulation. Years ago, before the development of modern insulating materials, a vapor barrier was necessary ev-

A single house may use several different types of insulation. In the drawing below, for example, a cutaway of an attic converted for living space shows mineral wool used for loose fill on the horizontal level behind the knee wall, fiber glass between the collar beams in the attic and in the slope above the knee wall, and polyurethane boards inside the knee wall.

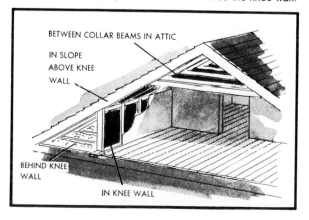

BETWEEN COLLAR BEAMS IN ATTIC

IN SLOPE ABOVE KNEE WALL

BEHIND KNEE WALL

IN KNEE WALL

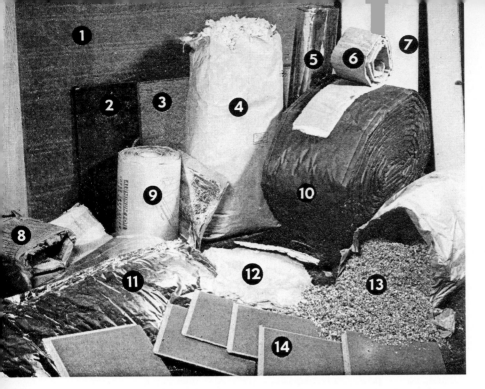

The first three numbered items, wood-fiber board, perlite board, and gypsum lined with aluminum have insulating qualities but are not sold as insulation. Real thermal insulating materials are: (4) loose-fill mineral wool, (5) aluminum foil, (6) sill sealer, (7) polystyrene and polyurethane boards, (8) mineral-wool blankets, (9) layered aluminum foil, (10) wood-fiber blanket sealed in plastic, (11) mineral-wool blanket sealed in aluminum, (12) mineral-wool batts, and (13) loose-fill vermiculite. Ceiling tiles (14) are strictly for sound insulation.

The floor under the eaves should be insulated, as shown below, left, to prevent escape of heat from the room below. In laundry rooms and bathrooms, where a great deal of moisture is generated, a vapor barrier—usually a heavy sheet of plastic—is required to keep the insulation dry. It is installed on the warm side of the insulation.

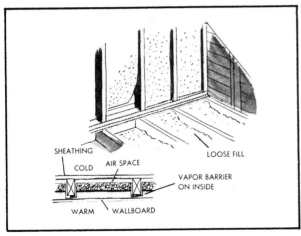

SHEATHING
LOOSE FILL
COLD
AIR SPACE
VAPOR BARRIER ON INSIDE
WARM
WALLBOARD

erywhere to prevent moisture formed inside the house from condensing on the walls, penetrating them, and dampening the insulation, which becomes ineffective when wet. Nowadays, however, it is sufficient to use a vapor barrier only where the moisture content in the air is excessive.

Sheets of polyethylene are made for this purpose. The plastic is installed behind the plumbing and wiring, between wall and insulation material, attached to studs. It should fit snugly around electrical outlets to prevent any moisture from passing through.

Insulation is sometimes thought to cause condensation on walls, but it does not. Moisture condensation can be a problem, however, even if you ventilate the laundry and bathrooms. Moisture can enter your house from the outside through leaky chimneys, crumbling mortar joints, leaky flashing, or loose siding or shingles. These troublemakers should be quickly repaired when discovered.

Insulating older houses

Fortunately, most houses on the market today are already insulated—fortunately, because to install insulation in a house that is already built is a big job. It can be done—you can hire a contractor with a machine for blowing mineral wool into the walls or one who is skilled in installing foam-in-place polyurethane—but it is an expensive undertaking.

As an alternative, you can remove the wall facings, put in insulation, and replace the wall—a messy job if your facings are plaster. You could also put gypsum wallboard lined with aluminum foil directly on top of existing walls, a much simpler operation of which the only drawback is that it reduces the interior

Light, fluffy mineral wool comes in large bags of loose fill, and you just pour it between the joists in flooring. Be careful not to step between the joists as you work; make walkways out of boards to get from one place to another.

Vermiculite is also installed by pouring the material between joists. Use plenty of the mineral and distribute it evenly by scraping with a T-square, which you can make by cutting square corners out of a piece of lumber.

If the joists are covered by flooring, you will have to remove sections of it to install insulation. Take up a few flooring boards at a time and push in insulation as far as possible with a wooden rake, a simple tool you can make yourself.

Reflective insulation is installed by stapling sheets of aluminum foil to studs, which is easy to do on vertical surfaces. Make sure the edges overlap so no heat escapes. Use one layer in warm climates, two or three in colder ones.

dimensions of the room to some extent and does not provide the quality of full insulation.

When adding a room or converting an unused room to a living area, be sure to insulate at the same time to save yourself future headaches. If, for example, you want to convert an attic that has been used only for storage into a bedroom or study, you will be starting with unfinished walls and exposed studs and joists. Insulation is installed in the manner shown in some detail in the illustrations on these pages.

You will note from these illustrations that insulating can be a relatively simple job which you are capable of undertaking yourself. After

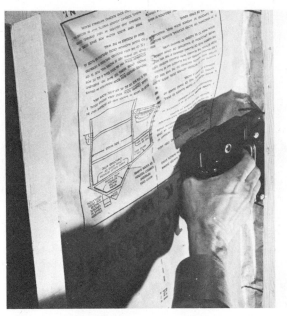

Mineral-wool and wood-fiber blankets come sealed in asphalt-coated paper or in plastic, both of which act as a vapor barrier. Edges of the sealing material have flanges which you can tack, staple, or glue to the edges of framing.

Make sure the ends of the blanket are attached securely at the top and bottom so it will not slip or work free. When you use insulation blanket in an attic ceiling between rafters, give it support over collar beams so it cannot sag.

Cut openings in the insulation to fit as snugly as possible around electrical outlets, and install the material behind the plumbing and wiring. Use same technique for the vapor barrier, which should be cut only when absolutely necessary.

To apply ceiling tiles, first attach wood furring strips to the ceiling joists in a grid pattern, then nail, staple or glue tiles to strips. Tiles are tongued and grooved so that nails or staples will not show on finished side.

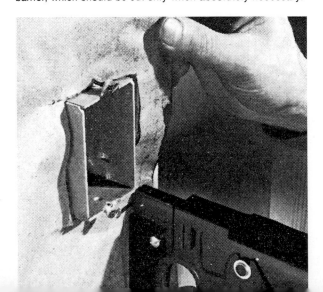

Before: A bleak, drafty attic that had been put to the usual use as storage area and junkroom. After most of the clutter had been cleared away, however, possibilities became evident: high ceiling and lots of space.

After: Because the floor area was large, the edges of the room were sacrificed and walls built to take advantage of the height in the middle. Stairwell is behind the built-in bench, and ceiling and walls have been insulated, tiled, and paneled.

the material is in place, apply wall facings and ceiling tiles or panels. The new room you have built will be as warm and as cozy as the rest of the house.

Finishing the attic

The first place most homeowners think of when planning an additional room for the house is the attic, where a shell already exists. It is easier to convert the attic, even though it may mean a ruthless clearance, than to add on a completely new room, constructing new flooring, walls, and roofing.

Nevertheless, if you have ever climbed into a storage attic in the dead of winter, you know it is too cold to be livable. The room may have a radiator, but most of the heat will escape if there is no insulation.

Before you begin work, however, there are a few things you should think about. One, do you need a permit from the buildings department of your city or town to make alterations? Two, can the existing floor support the weight

of a living area? Your joists must be sturdy enough and sufficiently closely spaced to take the load that builders figure necessary: 40 pounds per square foot minimum for residential floors; 60 pounds for the bathroom and laundry areas that must support heavy equipment. If you have any doubts, check with an architect, who will be able to tell you if the floor needs reinforcing. Locating a bathroom over another bathroom will take advantage of existing extra support and will simplify plumbing.

The third consideration: will the new room be useful enough to compensate for the time and money spent converting it? This may be a hard question to answer in advance; but if you don't ask it, you may find that you have an expensive white elephant on your hands.

On the other hand, you *can* turn space formerly used for clutter into a convenient, comfortable, and, best of all, completely private room. It is an excellent solution to space problems for a family whose children are

This attic room was converted into an extra living area for a young and growing family. Thermal-pane glass on the end wall both insulates and permits a wide view. Ceiling is insulated with fiber glass and faced with tile.

Below, left, ceiling tile is being fitted into place. Blanket insulation is fastened to studs behind the furring strips, which were nailed in criss-cross pattern to rafters. Tile slides into place and is stapled to furring. This tile has acoustical but not thermal insulating capacity.

Wall paneling is applied in a similar manner. Strips of 1 × 3s are nailed to studs on ten-, twelve-, and 16-inch centers, and facing material is placed on top. Positions of electrical outlets are first measured and marked, and material is finally cut to fit with a sharp knife.

growing older and need a place they can call their own, or for a family where grandparents come to live with them. In the new room the older couple can have all the privacy and independence to which they are accustomed.

If possible, add a bathroom to the floor plans; no apartment is really self-contained without one. A bathroom is one of the busiest rooms in the house—there never seem to be enough of them—and an extra one does wonders for preserving peace and good humor in a family.

Carpet the stairs leading to the attic. Stair carpeting is a safety factor, contributes to quiet, and helps make the new living quarters seem complete.

Tackling the job

An attic is exposed on four sides and the roof, which means that, unless you live in the Deep South, insulation is imperative. On the preceding pages the various kinds of insulation were described, with information about which to use for different applications—check that section before ordering materials. Plan to insulate all walls and the ceiling, and use the best insulation you can afford; more than any other area of the house, the attic will need it.

Once the insulation is in place—polyurethane, polystyrene, mineral board, or fiber fill in blanket form—nail wood furring strips to wall studs and ceiling joists. These will help keep the insulation in position, and will provide a base to which you can attach facing material of tile, paneling, or wallboard.

Arrangement of furniture in the attic room may call for more ingenuity than usual because of odd angles, sloping walls, and limited space. The attic is a place where the efficiency of built-ins is most obvious; and the irregularly shaped crannies and nooks may turn out to be an inspiration for cleverly designed shelves, cabinets, desks, or even beds. Decoration will also be a challenge, but even a simple coat of paint can produce a change more dramatic than in other rooms of the house. The section on guest rooms in this volume contains pictures of finished attics that show how the under-the-eaves space can be used to best advantage.

Weatherstripping

Even if your home is well insulated, cold air can seep in—and warm air leak out—through the spaces around windows and doors. You need weatherstripping, too. And you need it especially if all the doors and windows do not fit as snugly as they should. Because weatherstripping keeps out wind and wind-driven rain, which the overlaps built around the door and window frames are not likely to do effectively, weatherstripping can cut your heating bills as much as 20 percent above what you can save with insulation alone.

Weatherstripping is available by the foot or yard, or in kits with complete instructions. Installing it is an easy job, even for the novice homeowner—it can be done in an afternoon. But take enough time to do the job right. Check when finished to make sure that all doors and windows have been sealed and that the weatherstripping compresses somewhat when the door or window shuts. The fit should be a tight one.

There are three types of weatherstripping illustrated here: vinyl, polyurethane foam, and felt or other cloth types. There is also a new type on the market now which is excellent: neoprene. It is solid and resembles black rubber, although it is a synthetic. Of the other three types, felt or other cloth weatherstripping is the cheapest but it disintegrates more rapidly. Vinyl stripping is better, but it dries out in a few years and hardens so that it no longer cushions well. Polyurethane is considered the best and is the most expensive.

Your choice of material will, of course, depend on how much money you are willing to spend and what your individual requirements happen to be.

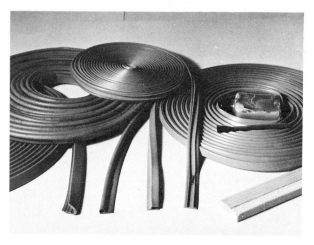

Variations of vinyl types of weatherstripping are, from left: friction-holding seal for metal sashes; a gasket type; sheath type for metal sash, requiring adhesive; a thin strip for the inner edge of a door; and a wood-vinyl foam strip.

Polyurethane foam types, from left: an 8-inch-wide adhesive-backed strip; a vinyl-covered polyurethane tube; and a ¼-inch foam with adhesive backing. Most of these come in colors to match interiors.

Felt and cloth types, from left: plain hair felt; wool and cotton felt combination; and a gasket type made of water-repellent fabric around a core of cotton. Sometimes the gasket comes with a rubber core instead.

How to Decorate and Operate
The Center and Heart of Your Home

In the late nineteen twenties theorists of modern architecture speculated about the function of the home and decided that if the house were a "machine for living" then the kitchen should look like a scientific laboratory for cooking.

Sterile white kitchens appeared across the country. They were uncomfortable and unattractive, but in those days the kitchen was often the domain of the servant girl—since servants were generally available—so how it was furnished did not seem too important. But now servants have just about disappeared. As the wit Saki wrote, "The cook was a good cook, as cooks go; and as cooks go, she went." Today the lady of the house is chief cook and bottle washer and the kitchen has once again become the heart and center of family living.

The following pages show you styles in kitchens and how to decorate them; how to use color; what flooring and countertop materials to choose from; how to treat windows and cabinets; how to solve the problems of small kitchens, of multipurpose kitchens, of odd-shaped kitchens. In Vol. 11, there are 46 pages of kitchen planning with floor plans, specific recommendations, detailed procedural steps for remodeling or building a new kitchen.

Charm and efficiency are now the main goals of kitchens. In a new or remodeled home, more care and planning are lavished on the kitchen than on almost any other room.

What style of kitchen you choose depends upon your personal preference, the size and habits of your family, and your available space.

The updated farm kitchen, left, combines modern conveniences with the charm of an old country kitchen. The circular island in the center serves several purposes; the top is used as a cooking-work-and-dining table, the space beneath is used for storage. The handcrafted copper shield holds a light fixture.

What delightful meals must be conjured up in this country ▶ kitchen, with its shiny white countertop and cleanly patterned blue-and-white tiles. Originally, the kitchen seemed cramped and dreary, but a few strokes of imaginative decorating revitalized it: Counter space was enlarged with the addition of a combined work and snack area; ornamental tiles on walls and floors brightened the area; and lighting fixtures added a note of practical elegance.

Dark-stained cabinets, heavy ceiling beams, and rough plaster walls—all basic and time-honored building materials—create an appealing country atmosphere. The rustic chandelier of roughhewn wood and wrought iron provides efficient modern lighting from its electric candles. A narrow strip of wall behind the stove is covered with vinyl paper decorated with designs of traditional blue-and-white Delft tiles. The black ventilator hood and the display of small copper molds are also reminiscent of country kitchens. The center island, with its butcher-block top, has drawers underneath and forms a convenient baking area. It has a recess on the sink side to allow room for sit-down jobs.

Country kitchens

If you like to cook over charcoal outdoors in fine weather, you can continue to roast and cook over firewood or charcoal in your kitchen when the weather turns cold if you provide a fireplace in the kitchen. However, some cooks say that twin ovens beat even a fireplace. Meal planning is simplified when you have two ovens and can cook one food at high heat and another at low heat simultaneously, or roast and bake at the same time.

Homeowners bent on having a country kitchen can sometimes rescue old materials and architectural details from a barn or house destined for the wrecking crew. Salvaging such treasures as old molding, cornices, or wrought iron hinges generally requires being at the right place at the right time.

There are other ways, however, to make a new country kitchen look impressively old. By using antique color stains, lightweight beams that appear to have been hand hewn, reproductions of early wrought iron hinges and handles, and rough-finished white plaster walls, the designer can produce a colonial look. Flooring of brick, tile, or flagstone is just right, and with the addition of a few early American accessories

Beams and shutters in the kitchen above were salvaged from old structures. They fit superbly into the modern room, and the heavy beam has been placed to help divide kitchen from dining room. Slate floor extends through both sections.

This closeup picture of part of the beam in the kitchen above right shows detail of delightfully carved bracket. A treasure like this is well worth a special salvaging trip.

Damaged headboard from discarded Jenny Lind bed was rescued and used to provide antique handles for cabinets: spool-turned spindles, sawed, sanded, and mounted.

you now have your old-fashioned kitchen — with all modern conveniences.

Using local materials

One of the best ways to produce a real country look in your kitchen is by using the materials that are indigenous to your area. Brick, field-stone, old barn siding, pine panels — all of these materials add rustic charm to a kitchen. But a kitchen need not look provincial even if you do use these materials. You can select contemporary furniture, accessories, and lighting fixtures to give your kitchen a clean, uncluttered, current look.

Remodeling

In the remodeled kitchen shown on these two pages, with its distinguished fireplace area for serving informal meals, many of the best features of planning are illustrated. The cooking space is relatively compact, but not crowded.

The angle of the sink counter brings it within easy reach of the wall oven at the far left and of the dishwasher under the adjoining counter. The planning desk fits neatly into the outer angle of the sink counter. This is where house-hold accounts are kept, and where business telephone calls are made. On the wall above is a bookcase for cookbooks. A storage cabinet in this spot would have been awkward to use, but the shallow bookshelf is easily accessible. Even the desk chair is versatile. When needed as an extra seat at the round table, it is merely turned around to face the table. The intercom control panel is placed logically near the phone.

One of the greatest benefits from remodeling the kitchen is that it adds to the value of the house. While it is rare to consider selling one's home as one plans to remodel and individualize it for family life, there is satisfaction in the realization that the kitchen adds future real value as well as daily convenience and pleasure.

The kitchen is generally one of the noisier rooms of the house and when remodeling the room it is usually worthwhile to install acoustical ceiling tile.

The colonial "keeping" room, or kitchen, always had a big fireplace. In this contemporary country kitchen, the fireplace is romantically big but most efficiently engineered. One half is low for burning logs and warming hearts and cockles; the other half is raised to convenient cooking height. Under the cooking surface is a bin for extra wood. The small bull's-eye windowpanes are a happy choice when one wants both light and privacy, or to use at a window with an unattractive view. No curtains are needed with this glass.

◄ Country styling is given to this kitchen by the brick wall and the red tile floor—with an additional gingham touch provided by the blue-and-white checkered counter. The blue-and-white color scheme is carried through in the chairs and the Formica desk surface, and in the antique plates displayed near the top of the wall and across a structural beam. The dominant expanse of rough brick adds textural interest and prevents the room from appearing too glossy. The flooring ties together the three areas—cooking, planning, and dining.

A country kitchen constructed of modern materials has one big advantage over the kitchen made with old beams, salvaged carvings, and wooden cabinets: it is easier to keep clean. Vinyl, Formica, and stainless steel are just a few of the helpful materials available.

Choose your kitchen flooring carefully. It is of the utmost importance to use a type of flooring that is impervious to alkalis or grease. Many floor covering materials made today meet these standards. Vinyl tiles, for instance, wear well, are easy to maintain, and come in designs that simulate many natural materials: travertine, marble, brick, and even wood. You can choose a design that is in keeping with the country look, but needing minimum care.

Garden fresh look

A country kitchen does not have to be modeled after a farmhouse kitchen. It can have a gay provincial look and still use only the most modern materials. For those who like informality, but do not want their pots and pans on view, there are a great variety of cabinets in bright colors or with provincial panelling or folk-art designs that *look* country but still conceal the paraphernalia of cooking and eating.

With the advent of epoxy paints anyone can indulge in a bright and colorful kitchen without waiting to replace the old refrigerator or dingy cabinets. Epoxy paints cover and cling to enamel without chipping; and there is a special epoxy for use on stoves — no matter how hot the oven and burners get, the paint does not blister or flake off.

This bright kitchen would have a garden-fresh air even if it happened to be in a town house or high-rise apartment building. Although large, it is arranged to save steps. The angled snack bar is used at mealtimes to set up the next course. Ease of maintenance is guaranteed by the use of vinyl on floor and countertops, stainless steel sinks, enameled cabinets. Since the housewife's most tedious chore is oven cleaning, a self-cleaning oven like the one in this kitchen pays off. By the turn of a switch the oven is cleaned safely, automatically, and economically.

Plenty of old-fashioned white in the kitchen above—but what a difference the red makes! Red, pure and emphatic, is at its reddest when used with bright white. The bold floral wallpaper, plastic-coated, is also used on the front of the cabinets.

While the kitchen at top is basically white splashed with red, the one at left uses white as a thin outline on blue cabinets. Wallpaper of brick design reverses the pattern: rectangles of white outlined in blue. Red floor is the only contrast.

Styling with color

For too many years in the past, kitchens, like bathrooms, were thought of in one-color terms —the one color being stark white. Nowadays, all inhibitions have been shed and kitchens are often the most colorful part of the house. Tough new paints, plastic counter tops, patterned vinyl wallpaper, tile floors, and all appliances are

A Mondrianesque color scheme like the one below takes careful planning. To devise such a scheme, buy a package of art paper containing sheets of many different colors and shift the various colors around on a table or the floor until you find a combination that seems right—quietly harmonious or boldly vibrant. In this corner, most of the panels are white, with just three colors added—red, yellow, and purple. The design is a good example of boldly dramatic effect attained through restraint and an eye for balance. Within this large pattern the ceramic wall tiles form a smaller pattern of black and white.

Variations on one color give the kitchen above a serene look—and since the color is yellow, a cheerful look as well. The bright yellow of the cabinets pales to beige on the walls above, and deepens to a golden brown on the wall.

available in an endless variety of colors and designs; and if the decorator must watch expenses, the simple application of contact paper can work wonders.

There is a certain danger in the new freedom of kitchen decorating; the homemaker who has worked for years in a dreary room of dead white walls and dingy linoleum might find the modern variety of choice bewildering. Remember that the kitchen should be designed and decorated with as much care and taste as any other room in the house.

Subtly striped paper on the ceiling, ranging from deep khaki to pale cream and gold, sets the color scheme for the rest of the room above. Wall cabinets repeat the cream, lower cabinets pick up the khaki, and the floor displays a generous expanse of gold. These colors are also mixed in the bead curtains on the rear window. Center work island has lower ledge for snacks.

Today's kitchen designer has tossed out all the unimaginative notions about how things ought to look. Islands for baking or cutting have suddenly appeared in the middle of the room; cleverly designed lighting arrangements have replaced the ugly ceiling fixtures of old; floors have been rescued from drab colors and timid patterns. The kitchen has been changed from a place where the housewife has to be to one where she wants to be.

The sun-yellow kitchen at right is as tonic as a day at the beach. Its monochromatic color scheme is subtly varied. Washable vinyl wallpaper, warm Spanish tile floor, glazed brick counter, and thick wood chopping board add variations of tone and texture. The cabinets are paneled with translucent golden glass, and hall glimpsed at rear has wall of golden pecky cyprus.

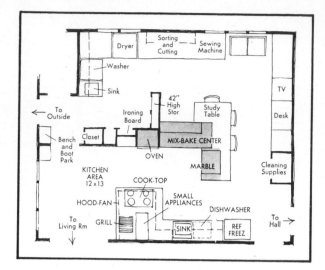

Diagram shows the layout of a room that contains almost ▶ everything needed for running a house. The space has been divided into compact working areas, each with its necessary equipment arranged in the most practical manner possible. Not many homes, perhaps, would be likely to have enough space available in one room for so many functions; but smaller rooms can be surprisingly multipurpose—and clever use of color can identify each area, yet tie all groups together.

A color-identified area

Color in a kitchen can be used to define areas as well as to cheer the soul. Large rectangles of color define the mix-bake area, right—the central area of the kitchen diagrammed above, This is a basic kitchen work center in its ideal form, organized for maximum efficiency—the sort of working space that would inspire the serious cook to new culinary triumphs. Everything she needs is at hand: plenty of counter space, with—a truly professional touch—a large slab of marble for rolling out dough; upper storage space with easy-to-reach shelves behind tambour doors; and deep storage below, with the heavy blender arranged to slide up and out without lifting.

Correct counter height is vital to minimize stress and strain. If you are remodeling, determine your best counter height for mixing and kneading: in your "kitchen" shoes, stand erect, drop your shoulders; bend your elbow, measure from elbow to floor, subtract 6 inches.

Food colors set the theme

Vegetables and fruits come in so many delightful colors that it seems quite logical to adopt the yellow of lemons, the purple of grapes, the red of apples, and the various greens of limes, lettuces, and string beans for decorating the kitchen. Oranges, tangerines, potatoes, squash —all of them have a distinct color that can be used effectively in a kitchen. These are the colors that make arrangements of food so photogenic and such a lure for the still-life artist—and that whet the appetite as well.

It is only in recent years that designers have agreed there should be no color taboos for the kitchen and that nothing is too good in the way of appliances, furniture, and accessories for this major room. Make the most of this new freedom—but settle on colors you'll be able to live with.

Country kitchens have always had a warm and lived-in look, but even they have never been as bright as many contemporary kitchens have become. And as color has moved into the kitchen, so have books (not just cookbooks), flowers, good pictures, and objects of art. Kitchen lighting, once garish, is now provided by concealed fluorescents or carefully placed ceiling fixtures.

◀ Spirited red streaks boldly across upper and lower cabinets, including dishwasher, in the kitchen at left, against a background of sparkling white. The giant blossoms on the wallpaper, always fresh behind a coating of vinyl, continue their kaleidoscopic pattern across the two panels of the refrigerator. An effective color scheme must show true at night, too; luminous panels guarantee cheerful general lighting.

Purple is the royal color, and it gives the kitchen above a truly regal appearance. Bold accents of citrus on the ventilating hood, and of olive on the floor, combine with the fresh color scheme of grape and white to give this room a one-of-a-kind look. The wide stripes of the vinyl flooring visually lengthen the small room. The books and handsome ornaments seem right at home in this elegant setting.

Black-and-white design of the wallpaper is repeated on the chair seats in the airy, light-filled kitchen-dining room above. Narrow wallpaper border subtly frames the triple windows; antique light fixture hangs above the table. Black handles on cabinets repeat graceful curves of floral design.

The dining area at right is around the corner from the kitchen ▶ area. The only items of kitchen equipment in this section are the rotisserie and its ventilating hood. Walls and cabinets are walnut, with cooking section made of same vinyl used on floor. Two ceiling spotlights illuminate the modern painting.

All-purpose kitchens

Many a busy woman feels that if her kitchen is large enough and efficient enough she can put up with any inadequacies in other parts of the house; small bedrooms, cut-up living room, no dining room—anything.

Even if a house is large, with plenty of rooms, there is much to be said for an all-purpose kitchen—a room where meals are prepared, laundry is washed, telephone and bill-paying tasks are accomplished; a room where children may do homework or where the family may occasionally watch television; and where everyone, including guests, dines.

Such a room must, of course, be large and extremely well organized. The dining area needs to have a certain elegance and kitchen cabinets should be both capacious and handsome.

Some multipurpose kitchens do not even look like kitchens at all. The functional workings

◄ In this all-purpose kitchen, left, the major appliances and cabinets are concentrated in an L-shape, freeing the rest of the kitchen for other activities. A desk with files makes a good place to write, pay bills, study recipes. At the near end of the kitchen is an octagonal Spanish-Moorish table with a sunken brazier in the center for cooking Chinese and Japanese dishes. Lanterns and the over-sink niche are also Moorish.

Family kitchens must be all-purpose rooms to function at top efficiency in today's homes. There is a traditional feel to the kitchen above, with its inviting hooded fireplace. The setting is reminiscent of provincial European and Early American kitchens, which were of necessity sitting and dining rooms as well as meal centers. The wooden ceiling with its heavy beams, the plaster walls, and the tile floor complete the mood.

may be concealed behind an island counter. The refrigerator may be so handsome it looks like a piece of furniture. Or the kitchen cabinets may be so stylish they look like built-in storage suitable for any room in the house. Instead of a range there may be a cooking counter with built-in storage underneath, and the oven may be wall-hung and camouflaged. In an apartment or a separate dining room or area such a kitchen can become a charming place for meals. The dining tables and chairs can be contemporary or of any period that suits the style of the kitchen. Usually the bright lights that are used for cooking and working can be dimmed or turned off while softer lights —or candles—are used for dining.

The kitchens of small apartments are often clearly visible from the living room; here again it is a good idea to decorate the kitchen so that it is camouflaged to a certain extent.

A party-food center is a sociable idea that is finding a place in many home plans, an arrangement that saves the hosts extra steps while entertaining. The party wall below is part of the kitchen. Its specialty—barbecued foods—can be cooked and served elegantly regardless of the weather. White countertop, black cabinets and hood, and gold hardware make the wall a handsome addition to the room.

A nonkitchen kitchen is one that operates so smoothly and is ▶ so attractive that no one even thinks of it as a work center. In the example at right, the high wall of the island shields appliances from dining view, and the sculptured white shapes of the chairs and table seem to float on the red carpet of easy-care nylon. Folding doors cover storage pantries beside the refrigerator-freezer. Chair upholstery is nylon velvet.

The small kitchen above utilizes all available space for cabinets above and below the counter. The table, though scaled to fit into the floor space without blocking traffic flow, is large enough for a cozy brunch for two.

Compact kitchen

Even if a kitchen is large, good planning organizes the major appliances into one section for the cook's convenience and sanity. Compact kitchens are efficient so long as there are enough working surfaces and storage cabinets. How much storage space is required varies with every family. Figure out what *your* needs are before planning your cabinets and be sure that some are deep enough to hold brooms, a vacuum, a waxer—if you store these in the kitchen. The best compact kitchens are open to other living areas.

This compact kitchen is organized to save steps as well as space in the placement of major appliances. The stove and the refrigerator/freezer are grouped against one wall with counter space between for a convenient work area, while the dishwasher is placed next to the sink in the central island, with work space above and behind it. Pots are hung decoratively from the ceiling fixture above the island.

Gourmet kitchens

One look at a kitchen and you can tell straight off if it belongs to someone who really loves to cook. Gourmet kitchens, no matter what their color scheme or general plan, will have certain things in common. Famed gourmet and cookbook writer Poppy Cannon says that two ovens help to produce good food. Since this is not always possible, she suggests augmenting one oven with a portable broiler-oven or a hot plate or hot tray.

André Surmain, creator and owner of the famous Manhattan restaurant Lutèce, says that a kitchen worthy of a good cook must have two sinks, plenty of counter space, and a ventilating hood over the stove. He prefers to have his pots and pans hanging up in plain sight and easy reach, and likes wooden kitchen counters so that he can slice and chop wherever he is working. He uses pegboards all over his kitchen walls for hanging spoons, forks, and knives. "I hate fumbling around in drawers," he says.

Julia Child, coauthor of the two-volume *Mastering the Art of French Cooking,* said on her television program that she insists upon having work counters and worktable high enough so that she does not have to stoop. Hers are higher than average, as she is rather tall. Her advice to a dedicated cook is to ignore the norm and insist on the comfortable height for oneself.

Craig Claiborne, food editor of *The New York Times* and author of *Kitchen Primer,* writes: "The most important thing in learning to cook well and with love is a sense of organization." For him, a gourmet kitchen must be carefully planned to suit the individual cook. He also says that a gas stove—the professional kind that restaurants use—provides highest heat and he likes it best of all.

Charlotte Adams, food consultant, editor, and cookbook author, suggests that spices be arranged in alphabetical order, that cooking wines be easily accessible, and that the refrigerator—a large one—be kept in neat order. "I clean up pots and pans as I go along," she says. "A blitzed kitchen is not necessarily the mark of a culinary artist."

In most kitchens designed to please a gourmet cook you will find individual touches, sometimes

The gourmet kitchen at right is intricate but workmanlike in its ▶ plan. Continuous counter, far right, serves as a buffet during parties. Its balanced lighting is especially effective: the cook never works in her shadow.

The same kitchen, left, is viewed from the opposite side. The heavy beams above call attention to the unexpected beauty of the floral-patterned cove ceiling. To show off the ceiling at night, fluorescent tubes were built into the beam tops. Beams and brick wall give country look to this kitchen.

even eccentric indulgences, which is as it should be. Cooking—dedicated cooking, that is—is a creative art, and few artists are the same. Some culinary exquisites like their French knives to be racked up on the wall; some like their ladles and spoons on a shelf at arm's reach. Some want a board where cheese can mellow—connoisseurs say better a banana than cheese in the refrigerator.

Carpets on the stone floor for easier standing; your best pictures on the walls; valuable ornaments on one or two shelves; a treasured chandelier for central lighting — whatever your whim may be, if you are one of the rapidly growing breed of loving cooks, indulge it in good health and with the full blessings of today's sympathetic gourmets.

The window area, above, of the kitchen at left has a large, double-bowl sink under the windows for heavy-duty work, and an auxiliary sink near the refrigerator for vegetable-washing convenience and for extra duty at party times.

Huge chopping block, right, extends beyond its storage base ▶ to create knee space for comfortable place to sit while working. The wide apron of stainless steel around the sink takes hot dishes from the oven or broiler. Behind this center unit can be seen another row of base cabinets—these with a top section of stainless steel containing four burners. A second sink is to the left, partly hidden by ceiling light. Dishwasher is set into cabinets, between burners and sink.

◀ Convivial kitchen at left uses craggy siding from weathered barns to give the ceiling an authentic old look. The electric ovens are encased in old brick—a design shape borrowed from pioneer homes. Trestle table serves as buffet and as counter for ovens. Natural quarry tile, set in random pattern, covers floor and counter. Plate rail spanning the wall cabinets holds collection of Meissen china.

An open grill brings the cookout season indoors for year-round pleasure. The ledge around the grill is ideal for keeping cooking utensils or sauces readily at hand. A fan in the exhaust hood whisks cooking smells and smoke out of the kitchen and is essential when cooking over an open coal fire.

Most cooks who love to cook are finicky about color in the kitchen: some say blue is depressing; some say red is too fiery; some do not like yellow. Just as many would vote for each of these as an honest, appetizing color to use in an inviting kitchen. The more time one spends in the kitchen, the more important it is to decorate it with colors that season your own gourmet soul. In short, if you are the cook, brew up your kitchen colors to suit your tastes just as you would an onion soup or a hollandaise sauce.

A roaring fire in the hearth sets the hospitable tone of this ▶ gourmet kitchen. The white-painted brick fireplace wall is extended to make room for the two wall ovens. The central work space, range, and grill are mounted on an oversize island, measuring 3 by 9 feet. The rest of the storage and work space is against the wall at the right. The floor looks like real French Provincial tiling but is a standard linoleum pattern, easy to care for and walk on. Pots hang overhead for impatient cooks to grab.

The kitchen above forms a closed U-shape that effectively bars traffic and saves steps for the cook while keeping her very much center stage. The floor is quarry tile and the countertops are made of soapstone, which must be sealed before it can be used for kitchen chores. To seal soapstone it should be varnished and then waxed. This ensures a rugged surface that can withstand chopping and cutting.

The counters in this kitchen, right, are made of tiles which ▶ have been treated with a durable glaze to protect them from spills. The spanking white tiles are easy to keep clean and give the kitchen a neat, crisp look. Colorful ceramic wall tiles are a decorative accent to the kitchen's brown and yellow color scheme. They too have been treated with a durable glaze to protect them from being damaged by splatters.

Cabinets and counters

The materials available today for use on counter tops and splash boards are diverse and often extremely decorative. Linoleum is a good choice —durable, attractive, available in a variety of colors and patterns. The recommended gauge for countertop use is 1/16-inch. Formica and other high-pressure laminated plastics resist stains, heat, abrasions, moisture, and fading. Suggested weight for countertops is 1/16-inch. Vinyl, available in various thicknesses, resists alcohol, stains, moisture, abrasion, and heat below 275°F. Ceramic tiles resist heat, water, stains, boiling liquids, and cuts. Small tiles are often mounted in groups on paper sheets. Stainless steel resists abrasion, will not chip, rust, or tarnish, but should not be used as a cutting surface. To avoid spotting, water and bleach should be wiped up promptly. Laminated hardwood is available in blocks, and resists heat below 382°F. Scratches may be eliminated by applying hot salad oil and letting it stand overnight. Although usually used only for making candy, marble is also excellent for countertops, being heatproof, durable, and moisture and stain resistant. (Oils do stain the surface, however.) Honed marble is best for countertops.

You can easily glamorize nondescript cabinets with new washable materials, as shown here. Apply the fabric over worn cabinets with paste formulated for vinyl wall covering. This tough covering is available in many colors, textures, and patterns. After it has been pasted on the front of the cabinet, trim the edges; then frame with narrow molding. Apply the molding with epoxy glue or tack it in place if the cabinets are wood. Remove hardware, of course, before beginning the covering job. Cabinets here are covered in various shades of wood-patterned vinyl; washable paper is used on the wall.

This kitchen was in good condition. There was ample floor ▶ space. The California sunshine came in by day. The lighting by night was satisfactory. With all of these pluses, the owners were still eager to have new counter tops and splash boards behind the stove and the cabinets. They chose ceramic tiles for both in brown-and-white checks that go well with the crewelwork wallpaper design. Unless one is experienced, ceramic tile is a job for a professional to undertake. The translucent roller shade is a white companion color to the handsome cabinets.

GLUE ⅛"x1" MOLDING

APPLY FABRIC
WITH VINYL
WALL PASTE

TRIM EDGE
WITH KNIFE

PLASTIC-COATED FABRIC

Creative kitchen cabinets

Take an ordinary kitchen, refurbish the doors of the storage cabinets, and the result can be a transformation of the whole room. The effect is often far out of proportion to the small amount of material and know-how required. Dramatic results can be achieved with just paper, scissors, and paste, plus the patience and care needed to do any job well.

For anyone with some artistic skill, a blank cabinet door can be as inviting as an empty canvas or a wall awaiting a mural. Depictions of flowers, vegetables, or herbs are appropriate for the kitchen; and if no one wants to attempt a freehand painting, choose some stencils from the endless variety available. If the doors have moldings around the central area, these can be treated as frames for the designs. If the doors are plain, moldings can easily be added.

When the paintings have dried, spray the doors with liquid plastic for waterproofing and for protection against smoke and grease. Once coated, your artwork will be easily washable.

Instead of painting, you might want to use the decoupage technique. Look through old magazines for pictures of appropriate subjects in appealing colors. When you have accumulated a good stack, remove the cabinet doors and arrange the pictures on the area to be decorated; then trace around them lightly so that you will be able to reposition them after brushing on the glue. Use white glue that is water soluble—it can be thinned if it thickens or lumps. When all the pictures have been glued in position, check for loose edges and allow them to dry. Then spray them with liquid plastic.

For an original and charming effect, bond antique molds of copper or tin to the doors with epoxy glue. These molds—the sort used for mousse or shaped jellies—can be found in amusing fish or animal designs as well as in the more conventional ring forms. Place them on the doors of the upper cabinets, high enough to avoid interfering with headroom.

For fabric inserts that match the curtains at the window, use wheat-type wallpaper paste to bond the fabric to flush wood doors. Let it dry overnight, then glue and tack cutout plywood panels over the fabric. Spray the cabinets with liquid plastic for long life and easy maintenance.

If you happen to be an artist as talented as the owner of this ▶ kitchen, you could turn your own kitchen into an art gallery. Each cabinet door is a framed painting, with the dominant colors of red, yellow, and black giving an Oriental look to the room. For the less talented, decoupage will give similar—if less impressive—results.

◄ The double-decker room divider, left, between the kitchen and dining area is accessible from either side and provides both storage space and a serving counter. Countertop, covered with mosaic tile, has a strip of chrome around the outer edge. Tne upper portion of the divider contains shelves for glassware. Plastic panels, tinted to look like golden bull's-eye glass, slide across the front. This "floating" cupboard is attached to steel bars on the ceiling by threaded rods covered with chrome tubing. The lower cabinet contains adjustable shelves and is made from prefinished paneling.

Previously, the kitchen below was a dark room with cramped space. It was enlarged incorporating a seldom-used back porch which was remodeled for permanent indoor use. This new area can be seen on the other side of the low, cushioned storage cabinet next to the chair. Plaster was stripped from one wall to reveal the red brick, and brick of the same color and rough texture was used to build the barbecue fireplace. Brick, wideboard panels, and rush-seated chair give the kitchen a rustic appearance. Floor is pine-colored vinyl, with a single row of patterned vinyl squares in front of the fireplace.

Remodeling

In remodeling a kitchen, there are several ways to cut down on the cost. One way is to do some of the work in the now time-honored American do-it-yourself way. The room on the facing page is the kind of kitchen that the home craftsman can construct. Its prefinished wood paneling is not difficult to handle. The wide choice of materials and finishes for kitchen walls, cabinets, and floors makes it easy to attain a custom-made look. Another way to cut down on expenses in remodeling is to be your own contractor. By buying the materials, hiring the workmen, and overseeing each job you can save a significant amount of money.

Pots and pans, brightly colored, can be made part of the decorating scheme in novel ways, as demonstrated in this kitchen. The brass pots and enameled colanders, too handsome to hide away, are hung on an iron ring suspended from the ceiling. A massive headboard has been salvaged to provide a spice shelf and a convenient place to hang towels and potholders. Its smiling sunburst repeats the dominant colors of the room.

This rustic kitchen demonstrates a successful blend of old and new. Modern appliances fit unobtrusively into country scheme of chestnut cabinets, plaster walls, brick floor, and rough overhead beams. The unique touch here is the display of the owner's collection of antique pewter on shelves between the windows.

Place it near the mixing center and thumbtack recipes to it for quick reference; or use it as a center for messages to and from other members of the family, or as a display board for your favorite photographs.

Is anyone in your family dieting? A small scale would be useful for weighing the precise amounts of meats and vegetables called for in many popular diets.

Whatever the idea, first plan your kitchen as an organized, efficient working place. Then add the touches that can give the room a bit of your own personality.

Kitchen ideas

While wallpaper and flooring are certainly important considerations, it is the small personalized touches that make your kitchen unique. An old filing cabinet can be rejuvenated with a coat of brightly colored enamel or gaily striped prepasted vinyl wallpaper that complements your color scheme; use it for filing everything from recipes to your children's report cards. A bulletin board can be attractive as well as functional, and is easily constructed by framing a sheet of cork with decorative molding to match the molding on your cabinet doors.

Not many kitchens have an expanse of glass like this, and the owner has made the most of it. Her green thumb has become a decorating asset, and the display of potted plants and herbs gives the kitchen an atmosphere of continual springtime. Old bottles of interesting color and shape are another distinctive feature.

The more our modern living-space contracts, the more the room designer's imagination must expand. Many older houses have large, poorly laid-out kitchens where a great deal of space is wasted; and even small apartment kitchens can be put to wider use than you might have thought possible. If your other rooms now seem to be as multipurpose as possible but you still seem short of space, cast a cold and calculating eye on the kitchen — you may suddenly realize it is not being used with maximum efficiency.

The major appliances should be organized into sensible groupings for the chief activities of cooking and dishwashing. Then organize other groups: laundering, formal dining, planning, studying, telephoning, games-playing, even television watching—all these activities can be carried on in the multipurpose kitchen. The dining table becomes a games table or a study desk; a typewriter and a telephone make a home office of one corner; a snack counter serves also as a room divider. The kitchen, once Siberia, becomes the most popular room in the house; and—paradoxically—our modern efficiency returns us to colonial days, when this room was the center of living.

This kitchen is dominated by a dramatically arched cooking alcove containing a barbecue and gas burners, with oven built into the easy-to-clean white glazed brick. Ceramic counter tops are used throughout, and the center of the room contains an island for cleanup and vegetable preparation. Breakfast area fits neatly under the windows.

A large kitchen is nothing to crow about unless it is planned ▶ for many activities. A room that is big just for the sake of being big simply adds steps between jobs. One area of this large kitchen, directly opposite the cooking and food preparation centers, is provided with a comfortable armchair, sturdy table, and shelves for TV, games, and books.

Mix or match patterns

When redecorating a kitchen it is usually a good idea to choose the patterned material first and then key all the paint colors to this pattern. It is often possible to find wallpaper and fabrics in the same design, but interesting effects can also be achieved by mixing different patterns that are color-keyed—stripes and floral patterns in the same shades, for instance; and sometimes a patterned paper on the ceiling will suit your decorating scheme.

Adhesive-backed vinyls are easy to use, but if the fabric you choose is not vinyl or is not plastic-coated it can be sprayed with liquid plastic for durability.

If you decide to use adhesive-backed paper or vinyl on the cabinet doors, mark its location on the doors with a template cut to match the lower corners of the door. Cut the panels to size and then separate the paper from its backing. Place the lower edge of the panel to fit the template mark, then press the panel against the cabinet surface. Work from center of panel to edges, gradually smoothing out the air bubbles.

The popular arch shape has been added to this kitchen by ▶ the use of cutout plywood over patterned vinyl. The vinyl on the cabinet doors is black with a white lattice pattern cleverly designed to give a three-dimensional effect. After the self-adhesive vinyl had been applied the plywood was glued on top. These pieces of plywood, with their cutout sections curved at the top, were painted green; then narrow white moldings were glued around their inner edges. This arch shape is particularly appropriate in company with the curved shape of the counter in this kitchen. Note also the black metal doorknobs designed in a circle of open loops. The section of wall above the window shows a pattern similar to the lattice design on the cabinets, and the green and white stripes of the woven roll-down blind add a third pattern. Curves, latticework, and stripes all combine well here.

Borders in a bamboo design have been applied to the cabinets above and below the sink, matching the bamboo design on walls and ceiling. Diagram below illustrates the technique. First, measure and cut a washable wallpaper border so pattern centers on each edge. Apply with wheat-type wallpaper paste, overlapping the corners. Cut mitered corner through both layers and then pull back corners to remove excess paper. Use a damp sponge to remove excess paste.

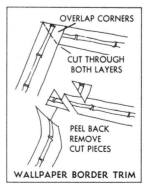

OVERLAP CORNERS

CUT THROUGH BOTH LAYERS

PEEL BACK REMOVE CUT PIECES

WALLPAPER BORDER TRIM

◄ Kitchen windows can be dressed up to be as charming as any others. Now that fabrics can be treated to resist soil, and with most stoves equipped with a ventilating hood, it is not impractical to use fine shades and fine curtain fabrics in the kitchen. In the kitchen at left, the boldly patterned blue-and-green wallpaper, the wide blue-and-white stripes of the Formica used on the counter and backsplash area, and the graceful brass pulls decorating the cabinets are all of note; but the piece de resistance is the elegant woven shade.

Closely related to two other areas—the adjacent dining room and the screened patio—the kitchen above is decidedly formal, with dark cabinets as nicely crafted as any furniture. The window treatment is in keeping with this formal theme: opulent gold curtains extend from ceiling to counter, and a geometric frieze marches across the upper part of the panes. Next to the door the curtains extend all the way to the floor, where their gold is repeated in the two rugs. Formality and opulence combine to make a truly pampering kitchen.

Kitchens with a view

An attractive kitchen interior is the result of careful planning, an eye for color, and a certain amount of hard work. Once in a while nature throws in a bonus—a beautiful view. Any homeowner lucky enough to live in scenic surroundings should make the most of his good fortune by using the view wherever possible as part of his decorating scheme—and this includes using it in the kitchen.

Wide expanses of glass are just the beginning: make a point of keying the room's colors to the natural colors outside, and avoid splashy pat-

terns. Consider changing the curtains with the seasons: cool blues or greens in the summer, warmer shades in the winter.

Changes in the outdoor colors are not just seasonal—sometimes they are hourly. The shifting patterns of light add subtle interest to a room of simple design.

The view may be dramatic—a desert landscape, a mountain range, a rocky coastline—or intimate—a small garden, a grove of trees, a brook; but whether the windows frame a panorama or a secluded nook, let the view work for you in your kitchen decorating.

Sky, mountains, desert, and sagebrush set the color scheme for this turquoise and pale yellow kitchen. The room has been kept simple and uncluttered—the only pattern is the muted plaid of the curtains. Extra window area means fewer cabinets, but efficient planning provides all storage space needed. Built-in bench is perfect place to lounge.

The view from this kitchen is less dramatic than the desert ▶ vista below, but the patterns of light and shadow on brick and wood, plus the glimpse of garden, add a great deal of charm to the room. Sliding glass doors and wide windows make the kitchen seem part of the sheltered patio outside, and the fresh green-and-yellow color scheme is keyed to the view.

Master/Guide

Gates

The parts of a fence or wall that open to permit entrance. For a discussion of construction, hardware, and decorative styles, see *Gates,* p. 1731.

Gaudreau, Antoine-Robert (c. 1680- c.1751)

A French furniture designer popular during the reign of Louis XV for whom he created several well-known pieces in the rococo style, such as the ornate commode still in the King's chamber at Versailles.

Gaudy Dutch Ware

Early nineteenth-century English pottery from Staffordshire marketed chiefly among the Pennsylvania Germans. The pottery was brightly and extensively painted.

Gauffre (or Gaffered) Fabric

The term applied to fabrics that have been calendered (or pressed) in such a manner as to produce embossments. The raised surfaces are not permanent and will wear away with time and washing.

Gazebo

A permanent but often delicate pavilion intended to embellish formal gardens and provide temporary shelter from wind, sun, or rain. In a more specific sense, the term is sometimes applied to the turret or gallery that appears on gazebos designed in a Victorian neo-Gothic style. For more information about traditional and contemporary styles, see *Gazebos,* p. 1738.

General Grant Style

An American architectural style that developed during the latter half of the nineteenth century. It was influenced by Greek Revival and neo-Gothic styles and produced eccentric and ostentatious structures upon which classic and Gothic motifs were awkwardly combined.

Genoa Plush

An Italian velvet featuring embossed floral patterns.

Genre Paintings

Paintings presenting ordinary people in ordinary situations. The execution of the genre painting is suited to the choice of subject matter: the field of vision is confined, the scale is small, and the figures are related in realistic proportions. Often, the paintings focus on tender or playful moments in domestic life. Despite these limitations, the genre style is exacting and capable of subtle and significant statements. In European painting, the genre style was brought to a high state of development by the Dutch in the seventeenth century, especially as exemplified by the works of Jan Vermeer, Gerard Terborch, Jan Steen, and Pieter de Hooch.

Jan Steen: The Feast of Saint Nicholas (c.1667); oil.

Georgian Furniture Styles

The general classification for the late Renaissance styles that prevailed in England from about 1715 through 1830, or during the successive reigns of the four Georges. The period is roughly divided into Early Georgian (1715-1750), Middle Georgian (1750-1770), and Late Georgian (1770-1810). The furniture of this period, although characteristic of late Renaissance styles, displays features that are distinctly English. However, after the Early Georgian rococo, the names of individual designers are better guides to identifying the styles of furniture, for it was during this period that Chippendale, Sheraton, and Hepplewhite produced their influential work.

German Porcelain

Chiefly hard-paste porcelain produced in the latter part of the eighteenth century. A German chemist, Johann Böttger, in 1708, discovered the process for making the first true hard-paste porcelain in Europe. The influence of the Meissen works, which he supervised, was greatly responsible for the technical brilliance of subsequent German porcelain. Principal factories were located in Meissen, Höchst, Nymphenburg, Frankenthal, Ludwigsburg, and Fürstenburg.

Gesso

Italian for plaster of Paris. Gesso, when thickly applied to a surface and allowed to dry, creates an excellent medium for delicate carving and, in this manner, it was often used in the decoration of furniture, especially in Italy and France. Gesso ornaments were also prepared from molds, applied to furniture, and then gilded or painted.

Gibbons, Grinling (1648-1721)

English carver and sculptor employed by Christopher Wren, particularly on the design and construction of St. Paul's Cathedral and Windsor Castle. His work is noted for its delicacy, complexity, and exacting realism, and is unsurpassed for its minute detail.

Gibbs, James (1682-1754)

English architect and furniture designer. His best-known architectural works are designed in the Palladian style popular after the death of Queen Anne.

Gilding

The practice of decorating objects or parts of objects either by means of powder or gold leaf (a thin sheet of gold). This kind of decoration, prized for its sumptuous effect, has been practiced since antiquity but was a favorite Renaissance mode of decorating furniture, ceramics, and metal works.

The Glynne Cup (c. 1590), gilded silver; Victoria and Albert Museum, London.

Gimp (or Guimpe)

A narrow tape or braid used in trimming upholstery or drapery. The material is often reinforced with wire threads. The term "gimp" also refers to the preparation of a stiff material used in embroidery.

Girandole (and Girandole Mirror)

An ornate seventeenth- and eighteenth-century candelabrum usually hung upon a wall in the manner of a sconce. The candle holders, either branching out and up from the wall plaque or standing upright from a projecting platform, were usually exquisitely designed bronze or silver. In the eighteenth century, the supporting wall plaque became a mirror, thus increasing the light provided by the girandole. This fixture was known as a girandole mirror. Later, any mirror that increased lighting intensity became known as a girandole.

Girder

A heavy horizontal beam used as a major support in the structure of a building.

Girls' Rooms

Rooms designed and furnished specifically to accommodate the tastes and activities of young girls. For more information, see *Girls' Rooms,* p. 1742.

Glass Wall Treatments

The treatment of large expanses of glass surface in home decoration. For suggestions and illustrations, see *Glass Wall Treatments,* p. 1752.

Glassware

A general term for glass objects used at the table. For information and illustrations, see *Glassware,* p. 1756.

Glaze

The glassy liquid coating (or its effect) applied to ceramics. The glaze is applied to a dry surface and then fused to the surface by baking. The effect thus produced can be either transparent or opaque, serving to decorate as well as protect the object. The chemical composition of the liquid varies, but the five major glazes are alkaline, lead, tin, salt, and feldspathic.

Gobelins

A dye and tapestry works founded in Paris by the Gobelins family during the fifteenth century. The works was purchased in 1662 by Louis XIV. Under his patronage, the Gobelins works flourished, producing Baroque tapestries of unique quality. The factory was closed during the French Revolution but reopened with the restoration of the Bourbons after 1814. It remains in operation today.

Goddard, John (1723-1785)

An American furniture designer who worked in Newport, Rhode Island, during the eighteenth century. His distinctive block-front furniture greatly influenced furniture design.

Gold Leaf

Very thin sheets of gold foil applied to surfaces for decorative effect.

Gondola

A term used to describe the arch-shaped, scoop-forming backs of some French Renaissance upholstered chairs and sofas. The curves of the arch continued to form the arms of the chair.

Gooseneck (or Swan Neck)

A steeply curved pediment broken in the center to form complementary scrolls or goosenecks on either side of the break. This pediment is often found on highboys and similar furniture.

Gothic Furniture Styles

The dominant styles of western Europe from the twelfth century until the gradual development of the styles associated with the Renaissance. The genius of the Middle Ages expressed itself most completely in the unique and compelling stone architecture of its religious centers, particularly the cathedral. Gothic furniture, however, was limited in kind and basically utilitarian. Domestic furniture was severe and simple: all-purpose chests and cupboards, stools and benches. Church furniture, however, was often beautifully and intricately carved and ceremonial articles were decorated with great skill. The decorative details of Gothic furniture were borrowed from architecture: carved foliage, arcading, figure subjects rendered in a grotesque mannner.

Gothic Revivals
The term for the periodic reawakening of interest in the styles of Medieval Europe. During the Early and Middle Georgian period, English designers such as Chippendale experimented with Gothic ornamental motifs, particularly on chairs and tables. Although this produced some interesting furniture, it had only a minor effect on the basic Renaissance mode of the Georgian style. Later, during the nineteenth century, Gothic styles were a major contributing influence in both architecture and church furniture.

Gouaches
Pigments soluble in water and used in a manner similar to tempera. If not excessively thinned, gouache exhibits some of the characteristics of oil paint. The term is also used to refer to paintings done in this medium.

Gouge Carving
A simple form of furniture decoration produced by chiseling out repetitive motifs with a gouge. The effect of gouge carving is similar to that of fluting or gadrooning. This decoration is usually found on English or Spanish furniture in a Gothic style.

Gouthiere, Pierre (1740-1806)
French metalworker (or *ciseleur*) famed for his craftsmanship and exquisite designs. Some of his best-known work was done for Madame du Barry.

Gout Stool
A Georgian footstool with a lid so constructed as to be easily raised and lowered at angles in order to alleviate the discomfort of a sitter afflicted with gout.

Graffiato (or Sgraffiato) Ware
Originally, heavy peasant pottery decorated with simple geometric motifs scratched into the surface. This form of pottery has existed since ancient times. In Renaissance Italy, however, pottery decorated with incised motifs and figures reached a high state of sophistication. The name *graffiato* is taken from the Italian, meaning "scratched."

Tuscan platter, mythical beasts incised under glaze.

Grandfather's (and Grandmother's) Clock
A pendulum clock housed in a tall wooden clock case which stands upon the floor in the manner of a narrow cabinet. A similar but smaller clock was known as a "grandmother's clock."

Grand Manner
In painting, a term used to describe an eighteenth- and nineteenth-century eclectic style given to large canvases or epic or historical subject matter rendered in an heroic manner.

Grass Cloth
A general term for materials made from vegetable fibers such as jute and hemp. These materials, often woven by hand, are durable but tend to wrinkle.

Grass Rug
An inexpensive floor covering made from vegetable fibers combined with cotton yarns. Sometimes the fibers are woven into squares and the

squares then are sewn together to produce larger units. Grass rugs are durable and attractive.

Grecian Furniture Styles

The furniture of ancient Greece, particularly the Grecian chair, or klismos, and sofa, or kline. Greek furniture, in form and decoration, stemmed from the culture of Asia Minor and Egypt. It was simple in form and limited in variety. However, it displayed the restrained elegance we associate with the classical world: graceful line, balanced structure, and simple but emphatic decoration. The klismos, the model for the neoclassic Empire and Federal sidechair, was without arms or upholstery. Its back curved in a concave, or klismos form, and the legs curved outward in the saber manner. In later adaptations of the klismos, the rear legs flowed in a continuous line to form the chair back. The kline, a couch used for dining and sleeping, was constructed in a lyre shape similar to the familiar Grecian sofa of the English Regency and American Federal periods. For a discussion, see *Classic Revival,* Vol. 5, p. 808.

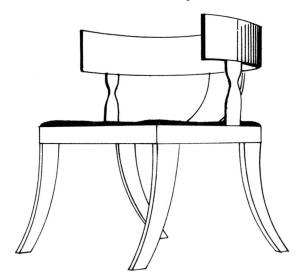

Greenhouse

An auxiliary building designed for the cultivation of flowers or vegetables in a controlled climate. For a discussion, see *Greenhouses,* p. 1764.

Griffin

An imaginary animal, half eagle and half lion, used in Greek and Roman ornamentation. The motif was revived as a carved ornament on Georgian furniture. The chimera and the sphinx were similar classical motifs.

Grille (or Grill)

Metal latticework often used in place of the main panel in cabinet doors or similar partitions. Curtains are sometimes hung behind the grille in order to enhance the decorative quality of the latticework.

Grisaille

Popular seventeenth- and eighteenth-century monochrome mural paintings, usually in tints of gray. The figures, often in classic poses and costumes, were rendered so as to give the illusion of low relief. Grisaille paintings were later applied to furniture, especially painted furniture designed by the Adam brothers and Thomas Sheraton. The term *grisaille* is derived from the French word for "gray."

Groin Vault

The vault produced by the intersection, at right angles, of two barrel vaults.

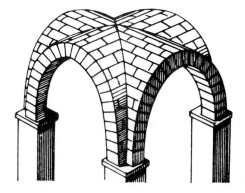

Gropius, Walter (1883-1969)

German architect who has profoundly influenced modern architecture and industrial design. Gropius was the founder of the Bauhaus, a school of design paramount in the formulation

Walter Gropius: The Fagus Works (1911-13); Alfeld, Germany. Designed in collaboration with Adolf Meyer.

of modern architectural styles. Gropius, as a teacher, was anxious to demonstrate that modern technology does not compromise the humanistic principles of Western culture.

Grosgrain
A heavy, ribbed silk fabric often used for formal clothing and ceremonial cloth. Grosgrain was popular in the court clothing of the Middle Ages.

Gros Point
Embroidery using wool or thread upon a net or canvas. The stitches are done in a diagonal manner across adjacent squares of the net. The techniques and the effect produced is similar to petit point. Gros-point needlework is often used in upholstery.

Grotesque
A Greco-Roman motif, similar to an arabesque in form and purpose, consisting of a band composed of half-human, half-animal figures bound together by filigree work. In a more general sense, the term is applied to any decorative motif featuring fanciful or bizarre creatures.

Guerite
A French hooded armchair usually of wicker construction and often used as an article of garden furniture.

Guest Rooms
Areas or rooms designed to accommodate guests. For more information about how to decorate and how to convert other areas to guest rooms, see *Guest Rooms*, p. 1768.

Guilloche
A decorative band composed of an intricate motif based upon circles interlocking in the manner of a chain.

Hadley Chest
An eighteenth-century American chest first made in the town of Hadley, Massachusetts. The chest, simply constructed and usually decorated

with overall incised and brightly painted floral designs, actually consisted of a chest with one or more drawers set beneath it. The top of this chest-bureau was formed by a hinged lid, permitting storage in the upper unit.

Half-Timber
A form of house construction characterized by a simple timber skeleton filled in with brick, stone, or plaster. The exposed timbers form a major portion of the decoration of the interior. The half-timber construction is typically English.

Half-Turning (or Split Spindle)
A carved post (or spindle) split lengthwise and then applied flat to a furniture surface as a decoration. This device is most typical of seventeenth-century Spanish, English, and American furniture.

Hallmarks
In gold and silver, a symbol or set of symbols used in the manner of a trademark to indicate the origin or maker. These marks vary greatly in kind and usefulness for identification purposes. For an illustrated discussion, see *Hallmarks,* p. 1775.

Hall Tree
A tall stemlike wooden or metal stand branching at the top in order to hold hats and coats. The hall tree was a common piece of furniture in Victorian entryways.

Hallway
A narrow entryway to a house or an area designed to function as an entryway. Hallway furnishings are varied and interesting in decorative possibilities. For a discussion of furnishings, see *Hallways,* p. 1776.

Hand Blocking
Printing fabrics by hand, using metal, wooden, or linoleum blocks to impress the pattern upon the material.

Handkerchief Table
A small, American corner table. The handkerchief table had three legs, a triangular top, and a triangular drop leaf supported by a swing leg when opened. The table derives its name from its resemblance to a folded handkerchief.

Hardanger Lace
An unusually fine, geometrically patterned lace made by hand in Hardanger, Norway.

Hardware (Decorative)
Metal fixtures, such as mounts, hinges, and drawer pulls, used in the construction of furniture and other furnishings. For a discussion of these, see *Hardware,* p. 1779.

Harewood
The wood of the sycamore tree, naturally green but usually dyed to a soft gray. Harewood was especially favored by eighteenth-century English cabinet makers.

Harlequin Table
An eighteenth-century English table with a lift-top lid and compartments for writing materials. When the table lid was raised, the compartments, by means of an ingenious mechanism,

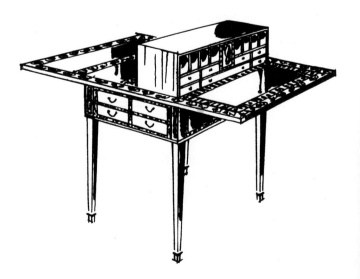

also raised. Since the table was equipped with drawers (and occasionally a mirror), it could serve as a dresser as well as a writing table. Any furniture designed to serve a concealed purpose was known as "Harlequin" furniture.

Harvard Chair

A three-legged, triangular armchair. The origin of this curious chair is Scandinavian. The chair derives its name from the fact that a chair of this kind has been used at Harvard graduation ceremonies since the seventeenth century.

Haviland China

Fine French china manufactured in Limoges and especially popular during the late nineteenth century. Haviland china was often decorated with delicate hand-painted floral motifs.

Headboards

The head section of a bedstead. For a discussion of styles and decorative treatments, see *Headboards,* p. 1784.

Heading

The term applied to any of the various kinds of decorative treatments, such as valances and swags, given to the tops of draperies. For examples, see *Draperies,* Vol. 7, p. 1224; and *Window Treatments,* Vol. 17.

Heating

Any of several domestic heating systems. For a discussion of relative merits, installation, and cost, see *Heating,* p. 1790.

Hemp

A textile fiber obtained from the outer bark of the hemp plant. The fibers are commonly used to make ropes, cloth, and inexpensive and durable floor coverings.

Hepplewhite, George (d. 1786)

Georgian furniture designer whose work is chiefly known through his design catalogue entitled

The Cabinet Maker and Upholsterer's Guide (published posthumously in 1788). The characteristic Hepplewhite design is light and neo-classic, emphasizing subtle and restrained ornamentation.

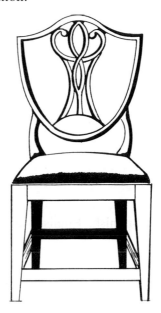

Herringbone Pattern

A furniture inlay band composed of strips of veneer in contrasting grains meeting at oblique angles in a feather-like pattern. The herringbone pattern was a popular motif on seventeenth- and eighteenth-century furniture.

Hickory

The wood of the native North American hickory tree. The wood is strong, yet elastic, and of a reddish brown hue.

Hi-Fi and Stereo

The abbreviated names for high-fidelity and stereophonic sound reproduction systems. For a description of the components forming these systems and the decorative possibilities of these components, see *Hi-Fi and Stereo,* p. 1792.

High Chair

A general term for a child's armchair with unusually long legs set at an angle to the seat in order to ensure the stability of the structure. The high chair has always been a common article of household furniture.

Highboy

A tall chest of drawers similar to the chest-on-chest or the tallboy. The highboy is formed in two distinct parts: a lower chest of drawers (resembling a lowboy) that rests (unlike the chest-on-chest) on legs of chair length, and an upper chest of drawers considerably taller and capped by an imposing pediment. The two sections are separated by decorative moldings. The highboy is English in origin and was introduced into America during the sixteenth century.

Hobby

Any pastime activity involving collections or creative relaxation. For a discussion of the decorative value of collections and the furnishings for housing these, see *Collections,* Vol. 5, p. 830; and *Hobbies,* p. 1800.

Hochst Porcelain

Hard-paste porcelain made in Höchst, Germany, during the late eighteenth century. The forms and decorative styles of Höchst porcelain are similar to those of other contemporary German porcelain centers: detailed and brightly enameled rococo figurines and tablewares.

Hogarth Chair (and Glass)

An eighteenth-century English chair with a distinctive double-curved back splat and heavy-kneed cabriole legs terminating in ball-and-claw feet. The chair receives its name from the fact that it often appears in pictures by William Hogarth. For the same reason, the artist's name is also given to a heavy-stemmed drinking glass.

Holloware

The general term for any vessel designed to hold liquids. The term is used in contrast to flatware. In a more specific sense, the term is applied only to silverware, such as creamers and teapots.

Holly Wood (Ilex aquifolium)

A hard wood of a white color often favored for inlays and marquetry. The wood is sometimes dyed black in order to simulate ebony.

Home Office

An area or room designed to accommodate a desk and other office furnishings for the conduct of personal business or hobbies. For information on how to design and decorate such areas, see *Home Offices,* p. 1804.

Homespun (and Tweed)

Originally, coarse and durable undyed woolen cloth woven on hand looms, particularly in the British Isles. Similar modern fabrics, although often labeled "homespun," are actually woven on power looms. Tweed (from the Scottish "tweel" or "twill") is a cloth similar to homespun.

Hoof Foot (or Pied De Biche)

A cloven or solid hoof terminating a chair or table leg. The hoof ornament was frequently used on the eighteenth-century cabriole leg, but it is an ancient ornament, found, for example, on Egyptian and Roman furniture.

Hooked Rugs

Colorful and durable rugs made by hooking narrow strips of cloth or yarns through a canvas or burlap foundation. For a discussion of tools and techniques, see *Hooked Rugs,* p. 1814.

Hoop (or Bow) Back

In a general sense, any chair back formed by a continuous arch, the ends of which are set into the chair seat. In a more specific sense, the term is applied to one style of Windsor chair that has a hooped back set into a horizontally curved arm rail, which forms part of the chair back.

Horsehair (or Haircloth)

A cloth woven from horse hairs (the tail and mane). Despite its coarse texture, horsehair was a popular chair or sofa covering in the nineteenth century.

Horseshoe Arch

The term applied to any arch design in which the sides are splayed, the arch thus forming more than a semicircle. This style of arch can be seen in Windsor chairs and various occasional tables such as the kidney or horseshoe writing table.

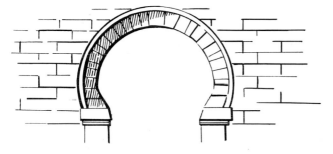

Hourglass (or Sand Glass)

A familiar though ancient timing device of two conical or pear-shaped glass parts joined at their mouths. A small channel in the constricted waist of the hourglass allowed fine grains of sand to pass from one part to the other. The size of the glass and the amount of sand it held determined the length of time that the hourglass measured. The hourglass cups rested in protective bases and the entire unit was often reinforced with spindles or thongs. The bases and the protective encasement varied greatly in decorative treatment and materials, ranging from wood and wrought iron to silver and ivory.

Housekeeping

The term used to refer to the techniques and tools used in general home maintenance. For a discussion of housekeeping tips, see *Housekeeping,* p. 1818.

House Plants

A general term for all plants and shrubs capable of flourishing indoors. For a discussion of their variety, care, and decorative assets, see *Houseplants,* p. 1820.

Hudson River School

A group of nineteenth-century American landscape painters generally related by stylistic similarities to Thomas Cole (1801-1848), whose large and romantic landscapes often focused on the Hudson River Valley. The best-known members of this group are Thomas Doughty, Asher Brown Durand, John Frederick Kensett, and Albert Bierstadt.

Hue

The term used in color terminology to refer to the color itself, such as a red hue or a violet hue. The term *value* refers to lightness or darkness of a hue. *Intensity* or *tone* refers to the brightness or dullness of a hue. For a discussion of these terms, see *Color,* Vol. 5, p. 842.

Hunter's Table (or Hunting Board)

An American sideboard of varied design and decoration, but characterized by its unusual height. The sideboard was generally used, particularly in the South, to serve buffets to the assembled sportsmen after the hunt.

Hurricane Lamp

A candle holder encased in a removable glass cylinder in order to protect the candle flame from drafts.

Hutch

An article of furniture evolving from the medieval chest. The term is used loosely to refer to a cabinet, often raised on legs, equipped with cupboards and drawers. In American colonial design, the hutch was a chair table equipped with a storage area beneath the chair seat. The term hutch is derived from the French *huche,* meaning "chest."

Imbrication

A decorative motif, either covering a surface in an extensive manner or applied to a molding, consisting of oval shapes overlaid in a manner suggesting fish scales. The motif originated in ancient Rome.

Impasto

The term used to describe the technique (and the effect) of applying an unusually heavy coating of paint to an area of a canvas in order to create texture or contrast. The technique has been variously used both in traditional and contemporary art, as, for example, in the work of the Venetian painter Titian (1477-1576) and the American painter Jackson Pollock (1912-1956).

Impressionism

A uniquely important late nineteenth-century French art movement. The impressionist movement departed from the academic assumptions and techniques of contemporary art and attempted to record, in a suitable technique, transitory and spontaneous moments or events, usually in an outdoor setting. They preferred bright color, diffused line, and vibrant shadow. The impressionist movement prepared the foundation for the critical acceptance of later and more radical innovations in painting. Cézanne and Renoir were two prominent impressionists.

Ince, William

Late eighteenth-century English furniture designer and cabinetmaker. Ince's designs were influenced by those of Chippendale, but they are distinguished by a tendency to a lighter line and more elaborate, delicate, and varied ornament.

Incised Lacquer

Furniture decoration formed by carving into a layer of lacquer. If the lacquer is applied to the furniture surface in layers of differing color, the carving can then expose the underlying color and thus produce the effect of polychrome.

India Print

Any cloth printed with a pattern suggestive of Indian ornamental styles. Indian prints are a wealth of colors and intricate patterns and are often used for casual clothes and decorative hangings and throws.

Inlay

An ancient form of furniture decoration, in technique and effect related to marquetry and mosaic. The patterns are created by cutting spaces into a surface and then filling the depressions with contrasting materials. This form of decoration was very popular in France and England during the eighteenth century. The materials used for the inlays were very diverse, including woods, metals, ivory, tortoiseshell, mother-of-pearl, marble, glass, and gems.

Insulation

The materials and techniques used in building to prevent the transfer of electric current, heat, or sound. For a discussion, see *Insulation,* p. 1852.

Intaglio

A carved or incised decoration sunk below the surface into which it is cut. Decoration in the intaglio mode is the opposite of relief, in which the decoration is raised above the surface. The printing process is known as gravure.

Intensity (or Tone)

In color terminology, the term used to describe the brightness or dullness of a hue. See *Color,* Vol. 5, p. 842.

Interlaced Chair Back (or Ribband Chair Back)

A chair back formed by a splat, crest, and sides carved to simulate interlaced ribbons. The ribband back was popular in eighteenth-century English and French designs and was illustrated in Chippendale's *Gentlemen and Cabinet Maker's Director* (1754). The spelling "ribband," used by Chippendale, is the eighteenth-century version of "ribbon."

Intermediate (or Tertiary) Color

In reference to the color wheel, a hue midway between a primary color and its complementary color. It can be formed by mixing a primary color with either of its nearest secondaries. For a more detailed discussion of these terms and an illustration of the color wheel, see *Color,* Vol. 5, p. 842.

Ionic

One of the orders of classical architecture. The Ionic order is distinguished from the Doric and Corinthian by the graceful volutes, or inverted scrolls, used as the primary decoration on the column capitals.

Iridescence

The free intermingling of colors in order to produce unique coloristic effects in glass and ceramics. This quality was particularly favored by late nineteenth-century glass designers and was exploited with unusual effectiveness by Louis C. Tiffany in the creation of Favrile glass.

Ironwood

Name applied in a general sense to any trees or shrubs that yield hard, heavy, and durable woods.

Italian Styles

Furniture distinctly Italian in structure and ornament. Italy, because of its close cultural and geographic relationship to the ancient world, never completely conformed to the Gothic styles that prevailed in northern Europe. Therefore, it was fitting that the Renaissance, the reawakening of interest in the past, should have first appeared in Italy. Italian Renaissance styles are commonly divided into four periods: the Quattrocento (1400-1500) or Early Renaissance, the Cinquecento (1500-1600) or High Renaissance, the Baroque (1560-1700), and the Settecento Rococo (1700-1750). After 1700, Italy's political history was dominated by forces outside the Italian peninsula and Italian styles reveal the influence of foreign tastes, especially

French, and the period revivals associated with northern Europe, such as Directoire and Empire. However, it is from Italy that the vital impulses of the Renaissance were transmitted to Europe and Renaissance furniture styles are primarily of Italian inspiration. For an illustrated discussion, see *Furniture Styles,* Vol. 9, p. 1626.

Baroque carved, gilded wood, Palazzo Pitti, Florence.

Ivory

The white, bone-like tusks of elephants and (in a broader sense) the horns or tusks of other animals, such as the rhinoceros, whale, and walrus. Because of its mellow color, rich surface, and suitability for carving, ivory has been used since ancient times in furniture construction and decoration. Ivory carving itself is an ancient, universal, and highly sophisticated art.

Jacobean Styles

The general term for the furniture styles that prevailed in England during the seventeenth century, or roughly, from the ascendance of the

Stuarts (James I) through the period of Cromwell to the Stuart Restoration in 1688. Furniture was bold, rectilinear, and austere, but often richly and skillfully carved. Later Jacobean furniture shows signs of French influence in lighter lines and more sophisticated decoration. See *English Styles,* Vol. 7, p. 1266, and *Furniture Styles,* Vol. 9, p. 1626.

Jacquard

A complex weaving technique named after the nineteenth-century French inventor, Joseph Marie Jacquard. By means of punched cards, Jacquard weaving allowed greater freedom in patterns and revolutionized the production of figured fabrics.

Japanning

The art of producing colored surfaces of a deep luster on wood, metal, or similar materials by the application of baked varnishes. The art originated in the Orient and became popular in Europe during the seventeenth century.

Jardiniere

Any article of furniture designed to contain plants or shrubs, either indoors or outdoors. The name derives from the French word for garden. See *Garden Rooms,* Vol. 9, p. 1706.

Joint (or Joined) Stool

A traditional English rectangular stool with four turned legs and stretcher bars. The pieces of the stool were fitted, or "joined," together, rather than glued or nailed.

Jones, Inigo (1573-1652)

Renowned English architect and furniture designer, who introduced to English architecture the principles of classic design as interpreted by the Italian architect Palladio.

Jouy

Originally, a French printed cotton fabric produced at Jouy near Paris. The prints were usually classical motifs designed in a realistic manner. Jouy was popular as a decorative fabric during the nineteenth century.

Kapok

The name for a filler, resembling a combination of silk and cotton, made from the fibers found in the seeds of the kapok tree and used primarily as filling for mattresses, pillows, and sleeping bags and as insulation.

Kas

A wide and tall wooden Dutch cabinet or cupboard usually topped by a cornice. The kas sat on squat ball feet in front and plain stiles in back and was ornamented with bold carving or paintings. Dutch settlers brought the kas to America and examples can still be found in the areas of the original Dutch settlements.

Kent, William (1685-1748)

English painter, architect, and furniture designer. Kent is considered among the first to attempt on a large scale to relate furnishings to architectural design in a coordinated manner. His architectural designs are influenced by Palladio as interpreted by Inigo Jones. His furniture designs are distinguished by ornate baroque ornamentation.

Kettle Shape

A term used interchangeably with the French *bombé* and applied to furniture with bulging front and sides as in the bombé commode.

Kidney Table

An eighteenth-century writing or working table in a bulbous horseshoe, or kidney, shape. In French furniture, this kind of table was known as a *haricot* (or kidney bean) table.

Kitchen

An area or room designed for cooking, storing, and serving food. For a discussion of design and decoration, see *Kitchens,* p. 1860, and Vol. 11.